taste of home.
Simply
Italian

182 Reasons to Say "Mangia!"

"Let's eat!" That's what you'll hear when the robust, flavorful fare from *Simply Italian* is on the menu. Showcasing a feast of traditional favorites, as well as contemporary new tastes, *Simply Italian* offers 182 mouthwatering recipes that prove cooking authentic Italian cuisine is not only possible, but simple!

From slowly simmered sauces and enticing antipastos to bubbly baked entrees and delectable desserts, *Simply Italian* offers a parade of richly satisfying Italian specialties.

To start things off, tempt dinner guests with savory appetizers such as garden-fresh Cilantro Tomato Bruschetta (p. 12), Italian Sausage-Stuffed Mushrooms (p. 13), Antipasto Stuffed Baguettes (p. 7) and more.

When more than a snack is in order, consider any of the hearty entrees such as Chicken Cacciatore (p. 76), Linguine with Fresh Tomatoes (p. 71) and Stuffed Shells Florentine (p. 42). Feeling adventurous? Then you'll love the updated twists on Italian classics, such as tender Tomato Gnocchi with Pesto (p. 58), gooey Broccoli Chicken Lasagna (p. 42) and scrumptious Chicken Orzo Skillet (p. 70).

There are dozens of enticing ideas for sandwiches, soups, breads, salads, side dishes and, of course, pizza! So whether you're craving a thick slice of Two Meat Pizza (p. 95), a comforting bowl of Pasta Fagioli Soup (p. 17) or a luscious slice of creamy Tiramisu (p. 104), you'll find it within the eight easy-to-use chapters: Appetizers; Hearty Soups & Sandwiches; Salads, Sides & Breads; Baked Pasta; Pasta, Noodles & Sauces; Meat, Poultry & Seafood; Pizzas; and Desserts & Beverages.

With *Simply Italian* the hardest part is deciding which dish to make first!

taste of home.
Simply
Italian

senior vice president, editor in chief: Catherine Cassidy
vice president, executive editor/books: Heidi Reuter Lloyd
food director: Diane Werner RD
senior editor/books: Mark Hagen
editor: Sara Lancaster
art director: Rudy Krochalk
content production supervisor: Julie Wagner
design layout artist: Nancy Novak
proofreader: Linne Bruskewitz
recipe asset system manager: Coleen Martin
premedia supervisor: Scott Berger
recipe testing and editing: Taste of Home Test Kitchen
food photography: Taste of Home Photo Studio
administrative assistant: Barb Czysz
cover photographer: Rob Hagen
cover food stylist: Alynna Malson
cover set stylist: Melissa Haberman

north american chief marketing officer: Lisa Karpinski
vice president/book marketing: Dan Fink
creative director/creative marketing: Jim Palmen

THE READER'S DIGEST ASSOCIATION, INC.
president and chief executive officer: Mary G. Berner
president, north american affinities: Suzanne M. Grimes

© 2010 Reiman Media Group, Inc.
5400 S. 60th St., Greendale WI 53129
All rights reserved.

Taste of Home is a registered trademark of
The Reader's Digest Association, Inc.

International Standard Book Number (10): 0-89821-806-3
International Standard Book Number (13): 978-0-89821-806-0
Library of Congress Control Number: 2010922329

Cooking, Caring, Sharing® is a registered
trademark of Reiman Media Group, Inc.

Printed in China
1 3 5 7 9 10 8 6 4 2

For other Taste of Home books and products,
visit ShopTasteofHome.com.

table of contents

appetizers. 4

hearty soups & sandwiches. 14

salads, sides & breads. 26

baked pasta 40

pasta, noodles & sauces 56

meat, poultry & seafood. 72

pizzas 84

desserts & beverages 96

index. 108

appetizers

calzone pinwheels / page 10

8

6

Tempt the taste buds with these snacks and starters. Whether you're hosting an elegant dinner, an informal get-together or a casual family event, these Italian-inspired nibbles will entice and delight.

rosemary cheese patties 6

tuscan kabobs 6

antipasto-stuffed baguettes 7

pesto chicken 7

pizza dip 8

cheesy mushroom morsels 9

rosemary veal meatballs 9

stuffed bread appetizers 10

calzone pinwheels 10

classic antipasto platter 11

pesto swirled cheesecake 11

stromboli slices 12

prosciutto bundles. 12

cilantro tomato bruschetta 12

herb mix for dipping oil. 13

fried cheese ravioli 13

italian sausage-stuffed mushrooms. 13

rosemary cheese patties

rosemary cheese patties

Prep: 25 min. + chilling / **Bake:** 20 min.

Judy Armstrong, Prairieville, Louisiana

We're a family that loves snacks, so I combined some of our favorite ingredients in this fast and scrumptious appetizer. Great for entertaining, it can be doubled and made ahead of time. Simply brown the patties just before guests arrive and serve with warm marinara sauce.

1	package (8 ounces) cream cheese, softened
1	cup grated Parmesan cheese
3/4	cup seasoned bread crumbs, *divided*
2	eggs
1-1/2	to 2 teaspoons minced fresh rosemary
1-1/2	teaspoons minced garlic
1/8	to 1/4 teaspoon cayenne pepper
2	tablespoons olive oil

Marinara sauce, warmed, optional

In a large bowl, beat the cream cheese, Parmesan cheese, 1/4 cup bread crumbs, eggs, rosemary, garlic and cayenne until blended.

Place the remaining crumbs in a shallow bowl. Shape heaping tablespoonfuls of cheese mixture into 1-1/2-in. balls; flatten to 1/2 in.-thickness. Coat with bread crumbs.

In a large skillet, brown patties in oil in batches over medium heat until golden brown. Drain on paper towels. Serve warm with marinara sauce if desired. **Yield: 12 servings.**

tuscan kabobs

Prep: 45 min. / **Broil:** 10 min.

Elaine Sweet, Dallas, Texas

With chicken, bacon, tomatoes and bread slices, this hearty appetizer is one all guests will clamor for. The red pepper aioli sauce provides a fantastic finishing touch.

16	bacon strips, cut in half widthwise
1-1/2	pounds boneless skinless chicken breasts
1	loaf (1/2 pound) French bread
32	fresh basil leaves
32	cherry tomatoes
1/2	cup lemon juice
5	tablespoons olive oil
1	teaspoon salt
1	teaspoon pepper

RED PEPPER AIOLI:

1	cup mayonnaise
1/2	cup roasted sweet red peppers
4	garlic cloves, peeled and halved
1/2	teaspoon crushed red pepper flakes

In a large skillet, cook bacon over medium heat until partially cooked but not crisp. Remove to paper towels to drain. Cut chicken into 32 cubes, about 1 in. each. Wrap a bacon piece around each cube. Cut bread in half lengthwise, then cut into 32 slices.

On 32 metal or soaked wooden appetizer skewers, thread a wrapped chicken cube, basil leaf, bread slice and cherry tomato. Place on baking sheets.

In a small bowl, combine the lemon juice, oil, salt and pepper; brush over kabobs. Let stand for 10 minutes.

Broil 3-4 in. from heat for 6-8 minutes or until chicken is no longer pink, turning frequently. Meanwhile, place aioli ingredients in a food processor; cover and process until blended. Serve with kabobs. **Yield: 32 kabobs (1-1/4 cups sauce).**

tuscan kabobs

antipasto-stuffed baguettes

Prep: 25 min. + chilling / **Bake:** 20 min.

Dianne Holmgren, Prescott, Arizona

These Italian-style sandwiches can be served as a snack or savored as a light lunch. A homemade olive paste makes every bite even more delicious.

- 1 can (2-1/4 ounces) sliced ripe olives, drained
- 2 tablespoons olive oil
- 1 teaspoon lemon juice
- 1 garlic clove, minced
- 1/8 teaspoon *each* dried basil, thyme, marjoram and rosemary, crushed
- 2 French bread baguettes (8 ounces *each*)
- 1 package (4 ounces) crumbled feta cheese
- 1/4 pound thinly sliced Genoa salami
- 1 cup fresh baby spinach
- 1 jar (7-1/4 ounces) roasted red peppers, drained and chopped
- 1 can (14 ounces) water-packed artichoke hearts, rinsed, drained and quartered

In a blender, combine the olives, oil, lemon juice, garlic and herbs; cover and process until olives are chopped. Set aside 1/3 cup olive mixture (refrigerate remaining mixture for another use).

Cut the top third off each baguette; carefully hollow out bottoms, leaving a 1/4-in. shell (discard removed bread or save for another use).

Spread olive mixture in the bottom of each loaf. Sprinkle with feta cheese. Fold salami slices in half and place over cheese. Top with the spinach, red peppers and artichokes, pressing down as necessary. Replace bread tops. Wrap loaves tightly in foil. Refrigerate for at least 3 hours or overnight.

Serve cold, or place foil-wrapped loaves on a baking sheet and bake at 350° for 20-25 minutes or until heated through. Cut into slices; secure with a toothpick. **Yield: 3 dozen.**

Editor's Note: 1/3 cup purchased tapenade (olive paste) may be substituted for the olive mixture.

pesto chicken

Prep: 35 min. / **Bake:** 30 min.

Taste of Home Test Kitchen

These tasty chicken bites feature a from-scratch pesto that's packed with robust Italian flavor. The versatile dish dreamed up by our home economists makes an equally wonderful snack or main dish.

- 1 cup loosely packed fresh basil leaves
- 1/4 cup minced fresh parsley
- 1/4 cup grated Parmesan cheese
- 1/4 cup olive oil
- 1 tablespoon pine nuts
- 1 to 2 garlic cloves
- 4 boneless skinless chicken breast halves (4 ounces *each*)
- 1/2 teaspoon salt
- 1/4 teaspoon pepper
- 2 tablespoons butter, melted

For pesto, combine the first six ingredients in a blender; cover and process until blended.

Flatten chicken to 1/4-in. thickness; sprinkle with salt and pepper. Spread each with 2 tablespoons pesto to within 1/2 in. of the edges. Roll up jelly-roll style, starting with a short side; secure with a toothpick or small metal skewer.

Place chicken in a greased 11-in. x 7-in. baking dish; brush with butter. Bake, uncovered, at 375° for 30-35 minutes or meat is no longer pink.

For an appetizer, cool for 15 minutes, then refrigerate until chilled. Cut cold chicken into 1/2-in. slices. **Yield: 12-16 appetizer servings or 4 main course servings.**

Editor's Note: To serve as a main course, remove toothpicks or skewers. Do not cut into slices. Serve warm.

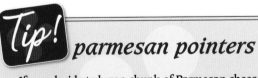

Tip! *parmesan pointers*

If you decide to buy a chunk of Parmesan cheese and grate your own, try using your blender or food processor. Cut the cheese into 1-inch cubes and process 1 cup of cubes at a time on high speed until finely grated.

pizza dip

Prep: 10 min. / **Cook:** 1-1/2 hours

Sara Nowacki, Franklin, Wisconsin

Everybody loves this simple, cheesy dip. If you have any left over, spoon it on toasted English muffins for a great open-faced sandwich.

- 2 packages (8 ounces *each*) cream cheese, cubed
- 1 can (15 ounces) pizza sauce
- 1 package (8 ounces) sliced pepperoni, chopped
- 1 can (3.8 ounces) chopped ripe olives, drained
- 2 cups (8 ounces) shredded part-skim mozzarella cheese

Bagel chips *or* garlic toast

Place the cream cheese in a 3-qt. slow cooker. Combine the pizza sauce, pepperoni and olives; pour over cream cheese. Top with mozzarella cheese. Cover and cook on low for 1-1/2 to 2 hours or until cheese is melted. Stir; serve warm with bagel chips or garlic toast. **Yield: 5-1/2 cups.**

cheesy mushroom morsels

Prep: 15 min. / **Bake:** 30 min. + standing

Marian Platt, Sequim, Washington

There's plenty of happy munching all around when I serve these luscious morsels. Ideal for a large crowd, they taste like quiche without the crust or the fuss.

1	pound fresh mushrooms, sliced
1	large onion, chopped
1/2	cup butter
1	large green pepper, chopped
2	garlic cloves, minced
10	eggs, lightly beaten
4	cups (16 ounces) shredded Monterey Jack cheese
2	cups (16 ounces) small-curd cottage cheese
1/2	cup all-purpose flour
1	teaspoon baking powder
3/4	teaspoon salt
3/4	teaspoon dried basil
3/4	teaspoon ground nutmeg

In a large skillet, saute mushrooms and onion in butter until tender. Add green pepper and garlic; saute 1 minute longer. Remove from the heat; drain.

In a large bowl, combine the eggs, cheeses, flour, baking powder, salt, basil and nutmeg. Add mushroom mixture. Pour into a greased 15-in. x 10-in. x 1-in. baking pan.

Bake, uncovered, at 350° for 30-35 minutes or until edges are golden and a knife inserted near the center comes out clean. Let stand for 15 minutes. Cut into squares. Serve warm. **Yield: about 12 dozen.**

cheesy mushroom morsels

rosemary veal meatballs

rosemary veal meatballs

Prep: 25 min. / **Cook:** 20 min.

Rhonda Maiani, Chapel Hill, North Carolina

These savory appetizer meatballs, seasoned with rosemary and garlic, get a touch of sweetness from chopped golden raisins. Using ground veal makes them extra tender and slightly more upscale for formal gatherings and special events.

1	cup (8 ounces) plain yogurt
1	jar (7-1/2 ounces) marinated artichoke hearts, drained and chopped
2	tablespoons prepared Italian salad dressing
1	garlic clove, minced

MEATBALLS:

2	eggs, lightly beaten
3/4	cup soft bread crumbs
1/2	cup golden raisins, finely chopped
3	garlic cloves, minced
4	teaspoons dried rosemary, crushed
1-1/2	teaspoons salt
1	teaspoon pepper
1	pound ground veal
1/4	cup canola oil

In a small bowl, combine yogurt, artichokes, salad dressing and garlic; cover and refrigerate until serving.

For the meatballs, in a large bowl, combine the eggs, bread crumbs, raisins, garlic, rosemary, salt and pepper. Crumble veal over mixture and mix well. Shape into 1-in. balls.

In a large skillet, brown meatballs in oil in small batches until no longer pink. Remove meatballs with a slotted spoon and keep warm. Serve with yogurt sauce. **Yield: 3-1/2 dozen (1-1/2 cups sauce).**

stuffed bread appetizers

Prep/Total Time: 20 min. + chilling

Tracy Westrom, Lansdale, Pennsylvania

You may want to double the recipe for this chilled loaf because I've found that folks just can't seem to stop eating it!

- 2 packages (one 8 ounces, one 3 ounces) cream cheese, softened
- 1 cup chopped celery
- 1 cup (4 ounces) shredded cheddar cheese
- 1/2 cup chopped sweet red pepper
- 1/2 cup chopped water chestnuts
- 1 teaspoon garlic salt
- 1 loaf (26 inches) French bread, halved lengthwise

Mayonnaise

Dried parsley flakes

- 4 dill pickle spears
- 4 slices deli ham

In a large bowl, combine the first six ingredients; set aside.

Hollow out top and bottom of bread, leaving a 1/2-in. shell (discard removed bread or save for another use). Spread thin layer of mayonnaise over bread; sprinkle with parsley.

Fill each half with cheese mixture. Wrap pickle spears in ham; place lengthwise over cheese mixture on bottom half of loaf. Replace top; press together to seal.

Wrap in foil; refrigerate overnight. Just before serving, cut into 1-in. slices. **Yield: about 2 dozen.**

stuffed bread appetizers

calzone pinwheels

calzone pinwheels

Prep/Total Time: 30 min.

Lisa Smith, Bryan, Ohio

Not only do these pretty bites take advantage of convenient refrigerator crescent rolls, but they can be made ahead and popped in the oven right before company arrives.

- 1/2 cup ricotta cheese
- 1 teaspoon Italian seasoning
- 1/4 teaspoon salt
- 1/2 cup shredded part-skim mozzarella cheese
- 1/2 cup diced pepperoni
- 1/4 cup grated Parmesan cheese
- 1/4 cup chopped fresh mushrooms
- 1/4 cup finely chopped green pepper
- 2 tablespoons finely chopped onion
- 1 package (8 ounces) refrigerated crescent rolls
- 1 jar (14 ounces) pizza sauce, warmed

In a small bowl, combine the ricotta, Italian seasoning and salt. Stir in the mozzarella cheese, pepperoni, Parmesan cheese, mushrooms, green pepper and onion. Separate crescent dough into four rectangles; seal perforations.

Spread cheese mixture over each rectangle to within 1/4 in. of edges. Roll up jelly-roll style, starting with a short side; pinch seams to seal. Cut each into four slices.

Place cut side down on greased baking sheets. Bake at 375° for 10-15 minutes or until golden brown. Serve warm with pizza sauce. Refrigerate leftovers. **Yield: 16 appetizers.**

classic antipasto platter

Prep/Total Time: 40 min.

Weda Mosellie, Phillipsburg, New Jersey

This large platter of sardines, anchovy fillets, cheese, olives and vegetables disappears quickly at every gathering.

- 1 pound fresh mozzarella cheese, sliced
- 1 jar (16 ounces) pickled pepper rings, drained
- 1 jar (10 ounces) colossal Sicilian olives, drained
- 4 large tomatoes, cut into wedges
- 6 hard-cooked eggs, sliced
- 1 medium cucumber, sliced
- 1 medium sweet red pepper, julienned
- 1 can (3-3/4 ounces) sardines, drained
- 1 can (2 ounces) anchovy fillets, drained
- 1/2 pound thinly sliced hard salami, prosciutto *or* smoked ham, optional
- 1/4 cup olive oil
- 1 teaspoon grated Parmesan cheese
- 1 teaspoon minced fresh oregano
- 1/8 teaspoon salt
- 1/8 teaspoon pepper

On a large serving platter, arrange the first nine ingredients; adding sliced meats if desired.

In a small bowl, whisk the oil, cheese, oregano, salt and pepper; drizzle over antipasto. **Yield: 14-16 servings.**

classic antipasto platter

pesto swirled cheesecake

pesto swirled cheesecake

Prep: 30 min. / **Bake:** 35 min. + chilling

Elizabeth Jackson, Portland, Oregon

This savory cheesecake was so popular at Thanksgiving, it was gone before my husband got a bite. Needless to say, he joined the appetizer line much faster when I made it for Christmas.

- 2/3 cup dry bread crumbs
- 5 tablespoons finely chopped pine nuts, toasted
- 2 tablespoons butter, melted

FILLING:
- 1 carton (15 ounces) ricotta cheese
- 1/2 cup half-and-half cream
- 2 tablespoons grated Parmesan cheese
- 2 tablespoons all-purpose flour
- 1/2 teaspoon salt
- 1/4 teaspoon garlic salt
- 2 eggs, lightly beaten

PESTO TOPPING:
- 1/2 cup loosely packed basil leaves
- 2 tablespoons grated Parmesan cheese
- 1 tablespoon pine nuts, toasted
- 2 garlic cloves, peeled
- 2 tablespoons olive oil
- Assorted crackers

In a small bowl, combine the bread crumbs, pine nuts and butter. Press onto the bottom of a greased 9-in. springform pan; set aside.

For filling, in a small bowl, beat ricotta, cream, Parmesan cheese, flour, salt and garlic salt until smooth. Add eggs; beat on low speed just until combined. Pour into crust.

For topping, combine the basil, Parmesan cheese, pine nuts and garlic in a food processor; cover and process until finely chopped. While processing, gradually add oil in a steady stream. Drop by teaspoonfuls over filling; cut through with a knife to swirl.

Place pan on a baking sheet. Bake at 350° for 35-40 minutes or until center is almost set. Cool on a wire rack for 10 minutes. Carefully run a knife around edge of pan to loosen; cool 1 hour longer. Refrigerate overnight. Serve with crackers. Refrigerate leftovers. **Yield: 24 servings.**

stromboli slices

Prep/Total Time: 25 min.

Rachel Jackson, Pennsville, New Jersey

I've served this dish several times, and at every occasion people have raved over it. Easy and mouthwatering, it's sure to please your party guests!

- 1 tube (11 ounces) refrigerated crusty French loaf
- 2 tablespoons olive oil
- 1/2 teaspoon dried basil
- 1 package (3-1/2 ounces) sliced pepperoni
- 2 cups (8 ounces) shredded part-skim mozzarella cheese
- 1 cup meatless spaghetti sauce, warmed

Unroll loaf of dough at the seam into a square; cut in half. Combine oil and basil; brush lengthwise down half of each rectangle to within 1/2 in. of edges. Layer brushed side with pepperoni and cheese. Fold plain dough over filling and pinch edges to seal. Place on greased baking sheets.

Bake at 350° for 10-15 minutes or until golden brown. Cut into slices. Serve the slices warm with spaghetti sauce. **Yield:** 1-1/2 dozen.

prosciutto bundles

Prep/Total Time: 40 min.

Gina Quartermaine, Alexandria, Virginia

Slices of salty prosciutto pair well with a lightly seasoned cream cheese filling in these bite-size snacks.

- 1 package (8 ounces) cream cheese, softened
- 1/2 cup minced fresh parsley
- 1 can (4-1/4 ounces) chopped ripe olives, drained
- 2 green onions, chopped
- 2 tablespoons finely chopped red onion
- 2 garlic cloves, minced
- 1/4 teaspoon pepper
- 16 thin slices prosciutto (about 10 inches x 3-1/2 inches)
- 32 whole chives

In a small bowl, beat the cream cheese, parsley, olives, onions, garlic and pepper until blended. Cut each prosciutto slice in half widthwise; place about 2 teaspoons of filling on the center of each piece. Bring up corners of prosciutto and tie with a chive, forming a bundle. Refrigerate until serving. **Yield: 32 appetizers.**

cilantro tomato bruschetta

Prep/Total Time: 25 min.

Lisa Kane, Milwaukee, Wisconsin

This easy, fresh-tasting bruschetta is irresistible and just the thing for spring and summer gatherings.

- 1 loaf (1 pound) French bread, cut into 1-inch slices
- 1/2 cup olive oil, *divided*
- 1 tablespoon balsamic vinegar
- 3 small tomatoes, seeded and chopped
- 1/4 cup finely chopped onion
- 1/4 cup fresh cilantro leaves, coarsely chopped
- 1/4 teaspoon salt
- 1/4 teaspoon pepper
- 1/4 cup shredded part-skim mozzarella cheese

Place bread on an ungreased baking sheet; brush with 1/4 cup oil. Bake at 325° for 10-12 minutes or until golden brown.

Meanwhile, in a small bowl, whisk the vinegar and remaining oil. Stir in the tomatoes, onion, cilantro, salt and pepper. Spoon about 1 tablespoon onto each slice of bread. Sprinkle with cheese. Serve immediately. **Yield: 12 servings.**

herb mix for dipping oil

herb mix for dipping oil

Prep/Total Time: 5 min.

Taste of Home Test Kitchen

Our home economists combined a blend of herbs to create this scrumptious mix. Plumping the herbs in water before stirring them into the olive oil enhances the flavor.

- 1 tablespoon dried minced garlic
- 1 tablespoon dried rosemary, crushed
- 1 tablespoon dried oregano
- 2 teaspoons dried basil
- 1 teaspoon crushed red pepper flakes
- 1/2 teaspoon salt
- 1/2 teaspoon coarsely ground pepper

ADDITIONAL INGREDIENTS (for each batch):

- 1 tablespoon water
- 1/2 cup olive oil
- 1 French bread baguette (10-1/2 ounces)

In a small bowl, combine the first seven ingredients. Store in an airtight container in a cool dry place for up to 6 months. **Yield: 3 batches (1/4 cup total).**

To prepare dipping oil: In a small microwave-safe bowl, combine 4 teaspoons herb mix with water. Microwave, uncovered, on high for 10-15 seconds. Drain excess water. Transfer to a shallow serving plate; add oil and stir. Serve with bread. **Yield: 1/2 cup per batch.**

fried cheese ravioli

Prep: 15 min. / **Cook:** 20 min.

Kate Dampier, Quail Valley, California

Be sure to make enough of these crispy ravioli appetizers. They're bound to be the talk of your party. The golden-brown pillows are so munchable when dipped in warmed tomato sauce.

- 1 package (9 ounces) refrigerated cheese ravioli
- 2 eggs
- 2 cups seasoned bread crumbs
- 1/2 cup shredded Parmesan cheese
- 3 teaspoons dried basil
- 1/2 cup canola oil, *divided*

Additional shredded Parmesan cheese, optional

- 1 cup marinara sauce *or* meatless spaghetti sauce, warmed

Cook ravioli according to package directions; drain and pat dry. In a shallow bowl, lightly beat the eggs. In another shallow bowl, combine the bread crumbs, cheese and basil. Dip ravioli in eggs, then in bread crumb mixture.

In a large skillet or deep-fat fryer, heat 1/4 cup oil over medium heat. Fry ravioli in batches for 30-60 seconds on each side or until golden brown and crispy; drain on paper towels. Halfway through frying, replace the oil; wipe out skillet with paper towels if necessary.

Sprinkle fried ravioli with additional shredded Parmesan cheese if desired. Serve ravioli with marinara sauce. **Yield: about 3-1/2 dozen.**

italian sausage-stuffed mushrooms

Prep/Total Time: 30 min.

Kelly McWherter, Houston, Texas

These hearty morsels are the perfect way to start an Italian-inspired feast. A savory sausage and cheese mixture is tucked into tender mushroom caps, then baked to perfection. It's almost impossible to eat just one!

- 32 large fresh mushrooms
- 1/2 pound Italian turkey sausage links, casings removed
- 4 ounces reduced-fat cream cheese
- 1/2 cup shredded reduced-fat cheddar cheese
- 1/4 cup thinly sliced green onions
- 2 bacon strips, cooked and crumbled

Remove stems from mushrooms and chop; set mushroom caps aside. In a small nonstick skillet coated with cooking spray, cook mushroom stems and sausage until meat is no longer pink; drain. Cool to room temperature.

In a small bowl, beat cream cheese until smooth. Add the cheddar cheese, onions and sausage mixture. Spoon into mushroom caps.

Place on a 15-in. x 10-in. x 1-in. baking pan coated with cooking spray. Bake at 400° for 20 minutes. Sprinkle with bacon. Bake 3-5 minutes longer or until heated through. Serve warm. Refrigerate leftovers. **Yield: 32 appetizers.**

hearty soups & sandwiches

tortellini soup / page 19

This dynamic duo truly is a match made in heaven. The freshest ingredients are stacked high or slowly simmered to create this mouthwatering collection of mighty sandwiches and flavorful soups.

italian sausage with peppers 16

garlic tomato soup 16

pasta fagioli soup 17

hearty sausage stromboli 17

hearty italian sandwiches 18

tortellini soup 19

barbecue italian sausages 19

italian beef sandwiches 20

italian wedding soup 20

prosciutto provolone panini 21

tuscan chicken soup 21

caprese sandwiches 22

focaccia sandwich 22

florentine chicken soup 22

forgotten minestrone 23

spinach meatball subs 23

meatball calzones 24

chicken alfredo stromboli 24

chicken tortellini soup 25

italian pork hoagies 25

monterey artichoke panini 25

italian sausage with peppers

Prep: 40 min. / **Bake:** 35 min.

Becki Clemetson, Sharpsville, Pennsylvania

Local fairs in these parts are famous for sausage and pepper sandwiches. I came up with my own recipe so our friends and family can savor these tasty treats anytime.

- 5 Hungarian wax peppers
- 1 large sweet yellow pepper
- 1 large sweet red pepper
- 2 medium sweet onions, chopped
- 2 tablespoons olive oil
- 1 can (14-1/2 ounces) Italian diced tomatoes, undrained
- 1 can (6 ounces) tomato paste
- 1/2 cup water
- 4 garlic cloves, minced
- 2 bay leaves
- 1 tablespoon dried parsley flakes
- 1/2 teaspoon dried basil
- 1/2 teaspoon dried oregano
- 1/2 teaspoon salt
- 1/8 teaspoon white pepper
- 8 Italian sausage links (4 ounces *each*)
- 8 hoagie buns, split

Seed wax peppers if desired; cut wax and bell peppers into 2-in. pieces. In a large skillet, saute peppers and onions in oil until tender. Stir in the tomatoes, tomato paste, water, garlic, bay leaves and seasonings; heat through.

Meanwhile, in a large skillet, brown the Italian sausage links. Transfer to an ungreased 13-in. x 9-in. baking dish. Top sausages with pepper mixture.

Cover and bake at 350° for 35-40 minutes or until a meat thermometer reads 160°. Discard bay leaves. Serve on buns. **Yield: 8 servings.**

Editor's Note: When cutting hot peppers, disposable gloves are recommended. Avoid touching your face.

garlic tomato soup

Prep: 30 min. / **Cook:** 30 min.

Marilyn Coomer, Louisville, Kentucky

Roasted garlic adds a mellow background to the rich, creamy flavor of this fresh homemade tomato soup. Canned tomatoes and tomato puree make it a year-round favorite.

- 12 garlic cloves, peeled and sliced
- 1-1/2 teaspoons olive oil
- 1 can (14-1/2 ounces) diced tomatoes, undrained
- 1 cup tomato puree
- 1 pint heavy whipping cream
- 1/4 teaspoon dried oregano
- 1/4 teaspoon minced fresh basil
- 1/4 teaspoon salt
- 1/8 teaspoon pepper

In a 3-cup baking dish, combine the garlic and oil. Cover and bake at 300° for 25-30 minutes or until lightly browned.

In a large saucepan, bring the garlic cloves, tomatoes and tomato puree to a boil. Reduce the heat; cover and simmer for 30 minutes.

Add the cream, oregano, basil, salt and pepper. Cool the mixture slightly. Place half of the soup at a time in a blender; cover and process until pureed. Return to the pan; heat through. **Yield: about 4 cups.**

garlic tomato soup

pasta fagioli soup

pasta fagioli soup

Prep/Total Time: 30 min.

Brenda Thomas, Springfield, Missouri

My husband enjoys my version of this soup so much, he won't order it at restaurants anymore. With fresh spinach, pasta and seasoned sausage, this fast-to-fix dish eats like a meal.

1/2	pound Italian turkey sausage links, casings removed, crumbled
1	small onion, chopped
1-1/2	teaspoons canola oil
1	garlic clove, minced
2	cups water
1	can (15-1/2 ounces) great northern beans, rinsed and drained
1	can (14-1/2 ounces) diced tomatoes, undrained
1	can (14-1/2 ounces) reduced-sodium chicken broth
3/4	cup uncooked elbow macaroni
1/4	teaspoon pepper
1	cup fresh spinach leaves, cut into strips
5	teaspoons shredded Parmesan cheese

In a large saucepan, cook sausage over medium heat until no longer pink; drain and set aside. In the same pan, saute onion in oil until tender. Add garlic; saute 1 minute longer.

Add the water, beans, tomatoes, broth, macaroni and pepper; bring to a boil. Cook, uncovered, for 8-10 minutes or until macaroni is tender.

Reduce heat to low; stir in sausage and spinach. Cook for 2-3 minutes or until spinach is wilted. Garnish with Parmesan cheese. **Yield: 5 servings.**

hearty sausage stromboli

Prep: 25 min. / **Bake:** 15 min.

Debbie Brunssen, Randolph, Nebraska

This stuffed loaf will get rave reviews from the whole gang. With a deliciously seasoned filling and tender Italian bread, what's not to love?

1/2	pound bulk Italian sausage
1/4	pound ground beef
1/2	cup chopped onion
1/2	cup sliced fresh mushrooms
1/4	cup chopped green pepper
1/2	cup water
1/3	cup tomato paste
2	tablespoons grated Parmesan cheese
1/2	teaspoon salt
1/4	teaspoon dried oregano
1/4	teaspoon minced garlic
1/8	teaspoon dried rosemary, crushed
1	loaf (1 pound) Italian bread
6	slices part-skim mozzarella cheese

In a large skillet, cook the sausage, beef, onion, mushrooms and green pepper over medium heat until meat is no longer pink; drain. Stir in the water, tomato paste, Parmesan cheese, salt, oregano, garlic and rosemary. Bring to a boil. Reduce heat; simmer, uncovered, for 5 minutes or until thickened.

Meanwhile, cut top third off loaf of bread; carefully hollow out bottom, leaving a 1/2-in. shell (discard removed bread or save for another use).

Line bottom half with three mozzarella cheese slices; top with sausage mixture and remaining cheese. Replace bread top. Wrap sandwich loaf in foil.

Bake at 400° for 15-20 minutes or until cheese is melted. Let stand for 5 minutes before slicing. **Yield: 6 servings.**

hearty sausage stromboli

hearty italian sandwiches

Prep: 20 min. / Cook: 6 hours

Elaine Krupsky, Las Vegas, Nevada

I've been making this sweet and spicy sandwich filling for many years. The seasoned meat mixture tastes just as good as it smells while it's cooking.

1-1/2	pounds lean ground beef (90% lean)
1-1/2	pounds bulk Italian sausage
2	large onions, sliced
2	large green peppers, sliced
2	large sweet red peppers, sliced
1	teaspoon salt
1	teaspoon pepper
1/4	teaspoon crushed red pepper flakes
8	sandwich rolls, split

Shredded Monterey Jack cheese, optional

In a Dutch oven, cook beef and sausage over medium heat until no longer pink; drain. Place a third of the onions and peppers in a 5-qt. slow cooker; top with half of the meat mixture. Repeat layers; top with remaining vegetables. Sprinkle with salt, pepper and pepper flakes.

Cover and cook on low for 6 hours or until vegetables are tender. With a slotted spoon, serve about 1 cup of meat and vegetables on each roll. Top with cheese if desired. Use pan juices for dipping if desired. **Yield: 8 servings.**

tortellini soup

Prep/Total Time: 30 min.

Karen Shiveley, Springfield, Minnesota

This rich and spicy soup brings a little Italian flair to your table. It's a nice recipe I invented after trying a similar version in a local restaurant.

- 2 packages (7 ounces *each*) pork breakfast sausage links
- 2 cans (14-1/2 ounces *each*) Italian stewed tomatoes
- 2 cups water
- 1 cup chopped onion
- 1/2 cup chopped celery
- 1 garlic clove, minced
- 1 teaspoon dried oregano
- 1/8 to 1/4 teaspoon cayenne pepper
- 1/8 to 1/4 teaspoon hot pepper sauce
- 1 bay leaf
- 3/4 cup refrigerated tortellini

In a 3-qt. saucepan, brown sausage; drain and cut into bite-size pieces. Return to pan; stir in the next nine ingredients.

Bring to a boil. Reduce heat; simmer, uncovered, for 15 minutes. Add tortellini. Bring to a boil. Reduce heat; simmer, uncovered, for 5 minutes or until pasta is tender. Discard bay leaf. **Yield: 8 servings (2 quarts).**

tortellini soup

barbecue italian sausages

barbecue italian sausages

Prep/Total Time: 30 min.

Taste of Home Test Kitchen

The tangy barbecue sauce used in this recipe is fast, flavorful and extremely versatile. It's fantastic on sausages, but our home economists suggest trying it on ribs or pulled pork, too.

- 4 uncooked Italian sausage links
- 1/2 cup chopped green pepper
- 1/4 cup chopped onion
- 1 tablespoon olive oil
- 1/3 cup dry red wine *or* beef broth
- 1/2 cup ketchup
- 1 tablespoon cider vinegar
- 1 tablespoon soy sauce
- 1 teaspoon brown sugar
- 1/4 teaspoon ground cumin
- 1/4 teaspoon chili powder
- 1/8 teaspoon Liquid Smoke, optional
- 4 hot dog buns, split

Grill sausages, covered, over medium heat for 5-8 minutes on each side or until no longer pink. Meanwhile, in a large skillet, saute green pepper and onion in oil for 3-4 minutes or until tender. Stir in wine or beef broth. Bring to a boil; cook for 2 minutes or until liquid is evaporated.

Stir in the ketchup, vinegar, soy sauce, brown sugar, cumin, chili powder and Liquid Smoke if desired. Bring to a boil. Reduce heat; simmer for 2-3 minutes or until thickened. Place sausages in buns; serve with sauce. **Yield: 4 servings.**

italian beef sandwiches

Prep: 20 min. / **Cook:** 6 hours

Keith Sadler, Oran, Missouri

After a very hectic day, our family loves coming home to the inviting aroma of Italian beef simmering in the slow cooker. I suggest using the broth from this recipe as an au jus sauce, perfect for dipping.

- 1 beef sirloin tip roast (2 pounds), cut into 1/4-inch strips
- 2 jars (11-1/2 ounces *each*) sliced pepperoncinis, undrained
- 1 small onion, sliced and separated into rings
- 3 teaspoons dried oregano
- 1-1/2 teaspoons garlic salt
- 1 can (12 ounces) beer *or* nonalcoholic beer

Mayonnaise, optional

- 8 hoagie buns, split
- 8 slices provolone cheese

In a 5-qt. slow cooker, layer the beef, pepperoncinis and onion; sprinkle with oregano and garlic salt. Pour the beer over the top. Cover and cook on low for 6 hours or until the meat is tender.

Spread mayonnaise on cut sides of rolls if desired. Place cheese on roll bottoms. With a slotted spoon, place meat mixture over cheese. **Yield: 8 servings.**

italian wedding soup

italian beef sandwiches

italian wedding soup

Prep: 30 min. / **Cook:** 45 min.

Noelle Myers, Grand Forks, North Dakota

I enjoyed a similar soup for lunch at work one day and decided to re-create it at home. I love the combination of meatballs, vegetables and pasta.

- 2 eggs, lightly beaten
- 1/2 cup seasoned bread crumbs
- 1 pound ground beef
- 1 pound bulk Italian sausage
- 3 medium carrots, sliced
- 3 celery ribs, diced
- 1 large onion, chopped
- 3 garlic cloves, minced
- 4-1/2 teaspoons olive oil
- 4 cans (14-1/2 ounces *each*) reduced-sodium chicken broth
- 2 cans (14-1/2 ounces *each*) beef broth
- 1 package (10 ounces) frozen chopped spinach, thawed and squeezed dry
- 1/4 cup minced fresh basil
- 1 envelope onion soup mix
- 4-1/2 teaspoons ketchup
- 1/2 teaspoon dried thyme
- 3 bay leaves
- 1-1/2 cups uncooked penne pasta

In a large bowl, combine the eggs and bread crumbs. Crumble beef and Italian sausage over mixture; mix well. Shape meat mixture into 3/4-in. balls.

Place the meatballs on a greased rack in a foil-lined 15-in. x 10-in. x 1-in. baking pan. Bake meatballs at 350° for 15-18 minutes or until no longer pink. Meanwhile, in a soup kettle or Dutch oven, saute carrots, celery, onion and garlic in oil until tender. Stir in the broth, spinach, basil, soup mix, ketchup, thyme and bay leaves.

Drain meatballs on paper towels. Bring soup to a boil; add meatballs. Reduce heat; simmer, uncovered, for 30 minutes. Add pasta; cook 13-15 minutes longer or until the pasta is tender, stirring occasionally. Discard bay leaves before serving. **Yield: 10 servings (2-1/2 quarts).**

prosciutto provolone panini

Prep/Total Time: 25 min.

Candy Summerhill, Alexander, Arkansas

For a quick lunch or supper, try this fancy, "up-town" take on grilled cheese sandwiches. They are fast and easy but still sophisticated enough for entertaining. I sometimes replace the fresh sage with 1 tablespoon Italian seasoning for a tasty variation.

- 8 slices white bread
- 8 slices provolone cheese
- 4 thin slices prosciutto
- 3 tablespoons olive oil
- 3 tablespoons minced fresh sage

On four slices of bread, layer a slice of cheese, a slice of prosciutto and a second slice of cheese. Top with remaining bread.

Brush both sides of sandwiches with oil; sprinkle with sage. Cook in a panini maker or indoor grill until bread is toasted and cheese is melted. **Yield: 4 servings.**

prosciutto provolone panini

tuscan chicken soup

tuscan chicken soup

Prep: 15 min. / **Cook:** 20 min.

Rosemary Goetz, Hudson, New York

Change up your traditional chicken soup by adding nutritious white kidney beans. It is also a great way to use up any leftover cooked chicken.

- 1 small onion, chopped
- 1 small carrot, sliced
- 1 tablespoon olive oil
- 2 cans (14-1/2 ounces *each*) chicken broth
- 1 cup water
- 3/4 teaspoon salt
- 1/4 teaspoon pepper
- 1 can (15 ounces) white kidney *or* cannellini beans, rinsed and drained
- 2/3 cup uncooked small spiral pasta
- 3 cups thinly sliced fresh escarole *or* spinach
- 2 cups shredded cooked chicken

In a large saucepan, saute onion and carrot in oil until onion is tender. Add the broth, water, salt and pepper; bring to a boil. Stir in beans and pasta; return to a boil. Reduce heat; cover and simmer for 15 minutes or until pasta and vegetables are tender, stirring occasionally. Add escarole and chicken; heat through. **Yield: 4 servings.**

Tip! *presentation pointers*

Adding a garnish to soup before serving gives color and adds to the flavor and texture. Easy ideas include finely chopped green onions or chives, minced fresh parsley, shredded Parmesan cheese or seasoned croutons.

Cut bread in half horizontally. Spread 1/4 cup spinach dip on each half; spread with mustard. Layer the turkey, cheese and tomato on bottom half; replace top half. Cut into wedges. **Yield: 10-12 servings.**

florentine chicken soup

Prep/Total Time: 30 min.

Cindie Henf, Sebastian, Florida

My husband loves Alfredo sauce, so I'm always looking for new variations. This easy-to-make dish is a wonderful way to use it. Pair the creamy soup with a loaf of Italian bread and a tomato and mozzarella-basil salad. It's the perfect meal for two.

- 1   cup uncooked penne pasta
- 1   package (6 ounces) ready-to-use chicken breast cuts
- 4   cups chopped fresh spinach
- 1   jar (7 ounces) roasted sweet red peppers, drained and sliced
- 3   fresh rosemary sprigs, chopped
- 1/2 teaspoon garlic powder
- 1/4 teaspoon pepper
- 1   tablespoon butter
- 1-1/2 cups reduced-sodium chicken broth
- 3/4 cup Alfredo sauce
- 3   tablespoons prepared pesto
- 2   tablespoons pine nuts, toasted
- 1   tablespoon shredded Parmesan cheese

Cook pasta according to package directions. Meanwhile, in a large saucepan, saute the chicken, spinach, red peppers, rosemary, garlic powder and pepper in butter until spinach is wilted. Stir in the broth, Alfredo sauce and pesto; cook for 4-5 minutes or until heated through.

Drain pasta and add to the soup. Sprinkle with pine nuts and cheese. **Yield: 5 cups.**

caprese sandwiches

Prep/Total Time: 15 min.

Stacey Johnson, Tacoma, Washington

We love this fast, fresh sandwich, especially when it's too warm to turn on the oven. I like to pair the layered bites with a fruity white wine and pasta salad or gourmet potato chips.

- 8   slices sourdough bread, toasted
- 1/4 cup wasabi mayonnaise
- 1/2 pound fresh mozzarella cheese, sliced
- 2   medium tomatoes, sliced
- 4   thin slices sweet onion
- 8   fresh basil leaves

Spread toast with mayonnaise. On four slices, layer the cheese, tomatoes, onion and basil; top with remaining toast. **Yield: 4 servings.**

focaccia sandwich

Prep/Total Time: 10 min.

Tina Miller, Sun Valley, Nevada

My family believes that nothing satisfies hunger like a hearty grilled sandwich, so I make them often for lunch, dinner and late-night snacking. They request this version often.

- 1   loaf (1 pound) focaccia bread
- 1/2 cup spinach dip *or* chive and onion cream cheese spread
- 2   tablespoons Dijon mustard
- 8   ounces thinly sliced deli smoked turkey
- 4   ounces slices Swiss cheese
- 1   medium tomato, thinly sliced

florentine chicken soup

forgotten minestrone

forgotten minestrone

Prep: 15 min. **/ Cook:** 7-1/2 hours

Marsha Ransom, South Haven, Michigan

This minestrone soup gets its name because the broth simmers for hours, allowing me to work on other things. But after one taste, you and your family will never forget the full-flavored soup packed with veggies and meat.

- 1 pound beef stew meat, cut into 1/2-inch cubes
- 1 can (28 ounces) diced tomatoes, undrained
- 1 medium onion, chopped
- 2 tablespoons minced dried parsley
- 2-1/2 teaspoons salt, optional
- 1-1/2 teaspoons ground thyme
- 1 beef bouillon cube
- 1/2 teaspoon pepper
- 6 cups water
- 1 medium zucchini, halved and thinly sliced
- 2 cups chopped cabbage
- 1 can (15 ounces) garbanzo beans *or* chickpeas, rinsed and drained
- 1 cup uncooked elbow macaroni
- 1/4 cup grated Parmesan cheese, optional

In a 5-qt. slow cooker, combine the first nine ingredients. Cover and cook on low for 7-9 hours or until meat is tender.

Add the zucchini, cabbage, beans and macaroni; cover and cook on high for 30-45 minutes or until vegetables are tender. Sprinkle each serving with cheese if desired. **Yield: 8 servings.**

spinach meatball subs

Prep: 20 min. **/ Cook:** 30 min.

Susan Corpman, Newhall, Iowa

These scrumptious subs star moist and tender meatballs prepared with a host of seasonings and spinach. Baked then topped with sauce and mozzarella cheese, the mouthwatering handhelds will soon become much-requested favorites.

- 2 large fresh mushrooms, quartered
- 2 tablespoons Worcestershire sauce
- 6 garlic cloves, minced
- 2 tablespoons Italian seasoning
- 1 teaspoon pepper
- 1/2 teaspoon salt
- 2 egg whites
- 1 package (10 ounces) frozen chopped spinach, thawed and squeezed dry
- 1/4 cup grated Parmesan cheese
- 1 pound lean ground beef (90% lean)
- 1 jar (14 ounces) marinara *or* spaghetti sauce
- 6 Italian rolls *or* submarine buns, split
- 6 tablespoons shredded part-skim mozzarella cheese

In a food processor, combine the first six ingredients; cover and process until blended. Add the egg whites, spinach and Parmesan cheese; cover and process until blended. Transfer to a large bowl; crumble beef over mixture and mix well.

Shape into 1-1/2-in. balls. Place meatballs on a greased rack in a shallow pan. Bake at 400° for 10-13 minutes or until meat is no longer pink; drain.

Place the marinara sauce in a large saucepan; add meatballs. Bring to a boil. Reduce heat; cover and simmer for 15 minutes.

Spoon meatballs and sauce onto rolls. Sprinkle with mozzarella cheese. Broil for 5-8 minutes or until cheese is melted. **Yield: 6 servings.**

spinach meatball subs

meatball calzones

Prep: 1-1/2 hours + standing / Bake: 25 min.

Cori Cooper, Flagstaff, Arizona

My family can't get enough of this satisfying entree. We have to have it at least once a month, or everyone seems to go through withdrawal. Leftovers freeze well for a quick meal later.

- 3   eggs, lightly beaten
- 1   cup seasoned bread crumbs
- 1   cup grated Parmesan cheese
- 3   teaspoons Italian seasoning
- 2   pounds ground beef
- 3   loaves (1 pound *each*) frozen bread dough, thawed
- 3   cups (12 ounces) shredded part-skim mozzarella cheese
- 1   egg white, lightly beaten
- Additional Italian seasoning
- 1   jar (14 ounces) spaghetti sauce, warmed

In a large bowl, combine the eggs, bread crumbs, Parmesan cheese and Italian seasoning. Crumble beef over mixture and mix well. Shape into 1-in. balls.

Place meatballs on a rack in a shallow baking pan. Bake, uncovered, at 400° for 10-15 minutes or until no longer pink. Drain on paper towels. Reduce heat to 350°.

On a floured surface, roll each portion of dough into an 18-in. x 12-in. rectangle. Spoon a third of the meatballs and the mozzarella cheese down the center of each rectangle. Fold dough over filling; press edges firmly to seal.

Place the calzones seam side down on greased baking sheets. Brush tops with egg white; sprinkle with Italian seasoning. Let stand for 15-30 minutes. Bake for 25-30 minutes or until golden brown. Serve calzones with warmed spaghetti sauce. **Yield: 3 calzones (4 servings each).**

chicken alfredo stromboli

Prep/Total Time: 25 min.

Tracy Haven, Henryville, Indiana

I combined my favorite fettuccine Alfredo dish with the chicken Alfredo pizza recipe from a nearby restaurant. The result was this filling, cheesy open-faced sandwich.

- 1   French bread baguette (5 ounces), halved lengthwise
- 6   ounces boneless skinless chicken breast, cubed
- 1   teaspoon olive oil
- 4   teaspoons butter, softened, *divided*
- 1/3 cup canned mushroom stems and pieces, drained
- 1/4 teaspoon salt
- 1/4 teaspoon garlic powder
- 1/4 teaspoon pepper
- 1/4 cup sour cream
- 1/4 cup grated Parmesan cheese
- 1/2 cup shredded part-skim mozzarella cheese

Place bread, cut side up, on an ungreased baking sheet. Broil 4-6 in. from the heat for 2-3 minutes or until lightly toasted; set aside.

In a small skillet, saute the chicken in oil and 1 teaspoon butter until the juices run clear; drain. Add the mushrooms, salt, garlic powder and pepper; cook for 1-2 minutes or until heated through.

In a small bowl, combine the sour cream, Parmesan cheese and remaining butter; spread over bread halves. Top each with 2/3 cup chicken mixture. Sprinkle with mozzarella cheese. Broil for 1-2 minutes or until the cheese is melted. **Yield: 2 servings.**

chicken alfredo stromboli

chicken tortellini soup

12 slices cooked pork (1/4 inch thick and
2 ounces *each*)
1/2 cup Italian salad dressing
1/2 cup shredded part-skim mozzarella cheese

e bottom and top halves of buns, cut side up, on an
eased baking sheet. Spread pizza sauce on the bottom
f each bun. Top with pork; drizzle with salad dressing.
le with cheese.

350° for 5-10 minutes or until the mozzarella cheese
d and the buns are lightly toasted. Replace the bun
ld: 6 servings.

chicken tort

Prep/Total Time

Jean Atherly, Red Lodge, Montana

*This simple idea is a fun Italian twi... ...ken
noodle soup. It's extra special made w... ...ortellini. The
blend of seasonings gives every bowl s...oonfuls of flavor.*

2 cans (14-1/2 ounces *each*) chicken broth
2 cups water
3/4 pound boneless skinless chicken breasts,
cut into 1-inch cubes
1-1/2 cups frozen mixed vegetables
1 package (9 ounces) refrigerated cheese
tortellini
2 celery ribs, thinly sliced
1 teaspoon dried basil
1/2 teaspoon garlic salt
1/2 teaspoon dried oregano
1/4 teaspoon pepper

In a large saucepan, bring broth and water to a boil; add
chicken. Reduce heat; cook for 10 minutes.

Add the remaining ingredients; cook 10-15 minutes longer
or until chicken is no longer pink and vegetables are tender.
Yield: 8 servings (about 2 quarts).

italian pork hoagies

Prep/Total Time: 20 min.

Jackie Hannahs, Fountain, Michigan

*I like to prepare these fast toasted sandwiches whenever I have
extra pork. I spread pizza sauce over hoagie buns before adding
sliced pork, Italian salad dressing and mozzarella cheese.*

6 hoagie buns, split
1/2 cup pizza sauce

...erey artichoke panini

Prep/Total Time: 25 min.

...s, Hartland, Wisconsin

*...a unique sandwich idea? This fresh combination of
...okes, spinach and fresh tomatoes will have you
... lips.*

4 slices sourdough *or* multigrain bread
4 slices Monterey Jack cheese (3/4 ounce
each)
1/2 cup water-packed artichoke hearts, rinsed,
drained and halved
1/2 cup fresh baby spinach
4 slices tomato
1 tablespoon butter, softened

On two slices of bread, layer a slice of cheese, artichokes,
spinach, two slices of tomato and remaining cheese. Top with
remaining bread. Spread butter on outsides of sandwiches.

Cook on a panini maker or indoor grill until bread is toasted
and cheese is melted. **Yield: 2 servings.**

monterey artichoke panini

salads, sides & breads

roasted garlic bread / page 37

They're the perfect way to round out an Italian feast. Freshly baked bread...crisp, green salads...flavorful side dishes...all the recipes you need to turn a meal at home into a memorable dining experience are right here.

fresh herb flat bread 28
antipasto picnic salad 28
italian spinach salad 29
italian broccoli with peppers 30
salami pasta salad 30
italian dinner rolls 31
parmesan romaine salad 31
tomato & olive bread 32
layered tortellini salad 32
antipasto salad with basil dressing 33
italian bread twists 33
antipasto medley 34
italian bread 35
pesto tortellini salad 35
easter bread 35
fresh mozzarella tomato salad 36
parmesan red potatoes 36
portobellos parmesano 36
roasted garlic bread 37
tuscan bean salad 37
super italian chopped salad 38
roasted vegetables 38
marinated pasta salad 38
basil-cheese bread strips 39
tuscan tossed salad 39

fresh herb flat bread

Prep/Total Time: 25 min.

Bev Credle, Hampton, Virginia

Since I grow so many herbs, I always look for opportunities to use them when I cook. This tried-and-true recipe features two of my favorites—basil and rosemary—but the savory loaf is also delicious using other combinations.

- 1   tube (8 ounces) refrigerated crescent rolls
- 1/4   cup fresh basil leaves, thinly sliced
- 1-1/2   teaspoons minced fresh rosemary
- 1   egg, lightly beaten
- 1   tablespoon grated Parmesan cheese

Unroll crescent dough and separate into two rectangles. On a lightly floured surface, roll each into a 10-in. x 7-in. rectangle, sealing seams and perforations.

Place one rectangle on an ungreased baking sheet. Sprinkle basil and rosemary to within 1/2 in. of edges. Top with remaining dough; pinch edges to seal. Brush with egg; sprinkle with cheese.

Bake at 375° 10-12 minutes or until golden brown. Cut into slices. Serve warm. **Yield: 10 servings.**

fresh herb flat bread

antipasto picnic salad

antipasto picnic salad

Prep: 30 min. / **Cook:** 15 min.

Michele Larson, Baden, Pennsylvania

No one can resist this tempting blend of meats, veggies and pasta. It goes together in no time, serves a crowd and tastes as scrumptious at room temperature as it does served cold.

- 1   package (16 ounces) medium pasta shells
- 2   jars (16 ounces *each*) giardiniera
- 1   pound fresh broccoli florets
- 1/2   pound cubed part-skim mozzarella cheese
- 1/2   pound hard salami, cubed
- 1/2   pound deli ham, cubed
- 2   packages (3-1/2 ounces *each*) sliced pepperoni, halved
- 1   large green pepper, cut into chunks
- 1   can (6 ounces) pitted ripe olives, drained

DRESSING:

- 1/2   cup olive oil
- 1/4   cup red wine vinegar
- 2   tablespoons lemon juice
- 1   teaspoon Italian seasoning
- 1   teaspoon coarsely ground pepper
- 1/2   teaspoon salt

Cook pasta according to package directions. Meanwhile, drain giardiniera, reserving 3/4 cup liquid. In a large bowl, combine the giardiniera, broccoli, mozzarella, salami, ham, pepperoni, green pepper and olives. Drain pasta and rinse in cold water; stir into meat mixture.

For dressing, in a small bowl, whisk the oil, vinegar, lemon juice, Italian seasoning, pepper, salt and reserved giardiniera liquid. Pour over salad and toss to coat. Refrigerate salad until serving. **Yield: 25 servings.**

Editor's Note: Giardiniera, a pickled vegetable mixture, is available in mild and hot varieties and can be found in the Italian or pickle section of your grocery store.

italian spinach salad

Prep/Total Time: 25 min.

Gloria Warczak, Cedarburg, Wisconsin

Here's a quick, colorful veggie salad that is as refreshing as springtime itself. The ingredients are simple, but the flavor is anything but ordinary.

4	cups fresh baby spinach
2	medium tomatoes, quartered
8	large fresh mushrooms, sliced
2	hard-cooked eggs, quartered
1/2	cup real bacon bits
1	small red onion, sliced and separated into rings
3	tablespoons snipped fresh dill
1-1/2	cups Italian salad dressing
1	teaspoon sugar
1/3	cup seasoned croutons

On eight salad plates, arrange the spinach, tomatoes, mushrooms, eggs, bacon, onion and dill. In a small saucepan, cook salad dressing and sugar over low heat until sugar is dissolved. Drizzle over salads; sprinkle with croutons. **Yield: 8 servings.**

italian broccoli with peppers

Prep/Total Time: 20 min.

Maureen McClanahan, St. Louis, Missouri

This healthy side dish goes well with just about any entree. We usually enjoy the garden-fresh medley over tender pasta or with grilled chicken.

6	cups water
4	cups fresh broccoli florets
1	medium sweet red pepper, julienned
1	medium sweet yellow pepper, julienned
1	tablespoon olive oil
1	garlic clove, minced
1	teaspoon dried oregano
1/2	teaspoon salt
1/4	teaspoon pepper
1	medium ripe tomato, cut into wedges and seeded
1	tablespoon grated Parmesan cheese

In a large saucepan, bring water to a boil. Add broccoli; cover and boil for 3 minutes. Drain and immediately place broccoli in ice water. Drain and pat dry.

In a large nonstick skillet, saute peppers in oil for 3 minutes or until crisp-tender. Add the broccoli, garlic, oregano, salt and pepper; saute 2 minutes longer. Add the tomato; heat through. Sprinkle with cheese. **Yield: 6 servings.**

salami pasta salad

Prep/Total Time: 20 min.

Sarah Ryan, Geneva, Ohio

The first time I tasted this delicious salad was at my wedding. I recall, even in the blur of that day, the recipe was in high demand. That was years ago and I'm still asked to bring the crowd-pleasing dish to cookouts and parties.

2	cups uncooked small pasta shells
3/4	cup chopped green pepper
3/4	cup chopped fresh tomatoes
1/2	cup chopped pepperoni
1/2	cup cubed hard salami
1/2	cup whole ripe olives, quartered
2	ounces provolone cheese, cubed
1/3	cup chopped onion
DRESSING:	
1/3	cup canola oil
1/4	cup red wine vinegar
2	tablespoons sugar
1-1/2	teaspoons salt
1-1/2	teaspoons dried oregano
1/2	teaspoon pepper

Cook pasta according to package directions; drain and rinse in cold water. Place in a large bowl; add the green pepper, tomatoes, pepperoni, salami, olives, cheese and onion.

In a small bowl, whisk the dressing ingredients. Pour dressing over pasta mixture; toss to coat. Cover salad and refrigerate until serving. **Yield: 9 servings.**

italian dinner rolls

italian dinner rolls

Prep: 20 min. + rising / **Bake:** 20 min.

Marie Elaine Basinger, Connellsville, Pennsylvania

Over the years, I've added a pinch of this and a dash of that to this recipe until my family finally agreed it was just right. These fluffy rolls are especially good served warm, right from the oven, with spaghetti and lasagna.

3-1/2	to 4 cups all-purpose flour
2	tablespoons sugar
2	packages (1/4 ounce *each*) active dry yeast
2	teaspoons garlic salt
1	teaspoon onion powder
1	teaspoon Italian seasoning
1	teaspoon dried parsley flakes
1	cup 2% milk
1/2	cup water
4	tablespoons butter, *divided*
1	egg
3/4	cup grated Parmesan cheese, *divided*

In a large bowl, combine 1-1/2 cups flour, sugar, yeast and seasonings. In a small saucepan, heat the milk, water and 2 tablespoons butter to 120°-130°. Add to dry ingredients; beat until moistened. Add egg; beat on medium speed for 3 minutes. Stir in 1/2 cup cheese and enough remaining flour to form a soft dough.

Turn onto floured surface; knead until smooth and elastic, about 6-8 minutes. Place in a greased bowl, turning once to grease top. Cover and let rest for 15 minutes.

Punch dough down. Turn onto a lightly floured surface; divide into 15 pieces. Shape each into a ball. Melt remaining butter; dip tops of balls in butter and remaining cheese.

Place in a greased 13-in. x 9-in. baking pan. Cover and let rest for 10 minutes.

Bake at 375° for 20-25 minutes or until golden brown. Remove from pans to wire racks to cool. **Yield: 15 rolls.**

parmesan romaine salad

Prep/Total Time: 20 min.

Karen Rahn, Hixon, Tennessee

The shaved Parmesan and nicely balanced dressing add intense flavor to this colorful salad. If you're pressed for time, you can use bottled Italian dressing.

4	cups torn romaine
2	cups grape tomatoes, halved
2	cups onion and garlic salad croutons
2	tablespoons lemon juice
1/2	teaspoon Dijon mustard
1	small garlic clove, minced
1/4	teaspoon salt
1/8	teaspoon pepper
1/4	cup olive oil
1	block (4 ounces) Parmesan cheese

In a salad bowl, combine the romaine, grape tomatoes and garlic salad croutons.

In a small bowl, whisk the lemon juice, mustard, garlic, salt and pepper. Slowly whisk in oil. Drizzle over salad; toss to coat.

Using a vegetable peeler, shave cheese into thin curls; sprinkle over salad. **Yield: 6 servings.**

parmesan romaine salad

salads, sides & breads

tomato & olive bread

Prep: 30 min. + rising / **Bake:** 15 min. + cooling

Ann Yarber, Goldsby, Oklahoma

I serve this savory yeast bread with spaghetti and meatballs or even a good steak. Pesto and ripe olives give this tender loaf a distinctive flavor that complements almost any meal.

1-1/8	teaspoons active dry yeast
1/4	cup warm water (110° to 115°)
1	tablespoon grated Parmesan cheese
1	tablespoon chopped ripe olives
1	tablespoon olive oil
1	tablespoon sun-dried tomato pesto
1	tablespoon egg white
2-1/4	teaspoons sugar
1/8	teaspoon salt
1	to 1-1/4 cups all-purpose flour

In a small bowl, dissolve yeast in warm water. Add the cheese, olives, oil, pesto, egg white, sugar, salt and 3/4 cup flour. Beat until smooth. Stir in enough remaining flour to form a soft dough.

Turn onto a lightly floured surface; knead until smooth and elastic, about 6-8 minutes. Place dough in a bowl coated with cooking spray, turning once to coat the top. Cover and let rise in a warm place until doubled, about 1 hour.

Punch dough down; shape into a loaf. Place in a 5-3/4-in. x 3-in. x 2-in. loaf pan coated with cooking spray. Cover and let rise until doubled, about 20 minutes.

Bake at 350° for 15-20 minutes or until golden brown. Remove from pan to a wire rack to cool. **Yield: 1 mini loaf (6 slices).**

tomato & olive bread

layered tortellini salad

layered tortellini salad

Prep: 30 min. + chilling

Nita Rausch, Dallas, Texas

My tempting tortellini salad combines layers upon layers of tastes and textures, and its colors are amazing. It's perfect for a salad luncheon or potluck. Consider using other cheese options such as Havarti, Fontina or Monterey Jack.

1/2	cup buttermilk
1/2	cup plain yogurt
1/4	cup mayonnaise
1	teaspoon sugar
1/4	teaspoon salt
1/4	teaspoon dill weed
1/4	teaspoon dried basil
1/8	teaspoon white pepper

SALAD:

1	package (9 ounces) refrigerated cheese tortellini
2	cups shredded red cabbage
6	cups fresh baby spinach
1	block (8 ounces) part-skim mozzarella cheese, cubed
1	cup cherry tomatoes, halved
1	small red onion, thinly sliced
8	bacon strips, cooked and crumbled
1/2	cup crumbled feta cheese

For dressing, place the first eight ingredients in a blender. Cover and process until blended; process 1-2 minutes longer or until smooth.

Cook tortellini according to package directions. Drain and rinse in cold water.

In a large glass bowl, layer the shredded cabbage, baby spinach and cheese tortellini. Top with mozzarella cheese, tomatoes, onion, bacon and feta cheese. Cover and refrigerate for at least 3 hours. Drizzle the salad with dressing; toss to coat. **Yield: 12 servings (1-1/2 cups dressing).**

simply **Italian**

antipasto salad with basil dressing

Prep/Total Time: 30 min.

Hunter Marlo, Blacksburg, Virginia

Serve this delectable mix of salami, veggie and mixed salad greens as an appetizer, side salad or a light meal. It's perfect for a family gathering or romantic picnic for two.

- 1 package (6 ounces) torn mixed salad greens
- 6 thin slices hard salami, quartered
- 1 jar (7-1/2 ounces) marinated quartered artichoke hearts, drained
- 1 large sweet red pepper, sliced
- 1/2 cup pitted Greek olives
- 1 small red onion, thinly sliced
- 1-1/2 cups (6 ounces) crumbled feta cheese
- 15 cherry tomatoes, halved
- 1/2 cup chopped walnuts
- 1 cup salad croutons

BASIL SALAD DRESSING:

- 1/2 cup olive oil
- 1/4 cup balsamic vinegar
- 5 fresh basil leaves, thinly sliced
- 1/2 teaspoon sugar
- 1/2 teaspoon garlic powder
- 1/4 teaspoon salt
- 1/4 teaspoon pepper

In a 3-1/2-qt. glass bowl, layer the first 10 ingredients in order listed. Cover and chill until serving.

In a small bowl, whisk the dressing ingredients. Just before serving, pour over salad; toss to coat. **Yield: 8 servings.**

antipasto salad with basil dressing

italian bread twists

italian bread twists

Prep: 30 min. + rising / **Bake:** 15 min.

Mary Gorman, Elliottsburg, Pennsylvania

These irresistible breadsticks and their pizza-inspired dipping sauce can be paired with most any meal. The aroma that fills the kitchen while they bake is absolutely heavenly.

- 2 to 2-1/2 cups all-purpose flour
- 1 package (1/4 ounce) quick-rise yeast
- 1/2 teaspoon salt
- 3/4 cup water
- 6 teaspoons canola oil, *divided*
- 1-1/2 teaspoons honey
- 2 tablespoons butter, melted
- 4-1/2 teaspoons grated Parmesan cheese
- 1 tablespoon dried parsley flakes
- 1/2 teaspoon garlic salt

PIZZA DIPPING SAUCE:

- 1 can (8 ounces) pizza sauce
- 2 tablespoons brown sugar
- 4-1/2 teaspoons cider vinegar

In a large bowl, combine 1-1/2 cups flour, yeast and salt. In a small saucepan, heat the water, 1-1/2 teaspoons canola oil and honey to 120-130°. Add to the dry ingredients; beat just until moistened.

Stir in enough remaining flour to form a soft dough. Turn onto a floured surface; knead until smooth and elastic, about 6-8 minutes. Cover and let rest for 10 minutes.

Roll into a 9-in. square. Cut into 1-in. strips. Twist each strip and place 2 in. apart on a greased baking sheet. Cover and let rise in a warm place until doubled, about 20 minutes. Combine butter and remaining oil; brush over dough.

Combine Parmesan cheese, parsley and garlic salt; sprinkle over dough. Bake at 350° for 15-20 minutes or until lightly browned. Remove to a wire rack.

Meanwhile, in a small saucepan, combine the dipping sauce ingredients. Bring to a boil. Serve with warm breadsticks. **Yield: 9 breadsticks.**

antipasto medley

Prep/Total Time: 30 min.

Bernadette Nelson, Arcadia, California

The enticing combination of beans, salami, cheese and pasta is a hearty complement to any meal and a welcomed addition to any gathering.

1	package (16 ounces) penne pasta
1	can (15 ounces) garbanzo beans *or* chickpeas, rinsed and drained
1	medium sweet red *or* green pepper, julienned
2	plum tomatoes, halved lengthwise and sliced
1	bunch green onions, sliced
4	ounces Monterey Jack cheese, julienned
4	ounces part-skim mozzarella cheese, juilenned
4	ounces brick *or* provolone cheese, julienned
4	ounces thinly sliced hard salami, julienned
3	ounces thinly sliced pepperoni
1	can (2-1/4 ounces) sliced ripe olives, drained
1	to 2 tablespoons minced chives

BASIL VINAIGRETTE:

2/3	cup canola oil
1/3	cup red wine vinegar
3	tablespoons minced fresh basil *or* 1 tablespoon dried basil
1	garlic clove, minced
1/4	teaspoon salt

Cook pasta according to package directions; rinse with cold water and drain. In a large bowl, combine the pasta, beans, vegetables, cheeses, meats, olives and chives.

In a small bowl, whisk the vinaigrette ingredients. Pour the dressing over the salad; toss to coat. Cover and refrigerate. Toss before serving. **Yield: 18 servings.**

italian bread

Prep: 20 min. + rising / **Bake:** 40 min.

Virginia Slater, West Sunbury, Pennsylvania

Years ago in Italian villages, bread was baked only once a week. So they made the loaves a little bigger to last for seven days. This crowd-pleasing recipe is a traditional favorite.

- 2 packages (1/4 ounce *each*) active dry yeast
- 3 cups warm water (110° to 115°), *divided*
- 3 tablespoons sugar
- 3 tablespoons shortening
- 1 tablespoon salt
- 1 egg, lightly beaten
- 8 to 10 cups all-purpose flour
- 1 tablespoon butter, melted

In a large bowl, dissolve yeast in 1/2 cup warm water. Add the sugar, shortening, salt, egg, remaining water and 4 cups flour; beat until smooth. Stir in enough remaining flour to form a stiff dough.

Turn onto a floured surface; knead until smooth and elastic, about 6-8 minutes. Place in a greased bowl, turning once to grease the top. Cover and let rise in a warm place until doubled, about 1 hour.

Punch dough down. Turn onto a lightly floured surface; divide in half. Shape each portion into a loaf. Place seam side down on greased baking sheets.

With a sharp knife, make four shallow diagonal slashes across the top of each loaf. Cover and let rise until doubled, about 1 hour.

Bake at 350° for 37-42 minutes or until golden brown. Remove from pans to wire racks to cool. Brush with butter. **Yield: 2 loaves (16 slices each).**

pesto tortellini salad

Prep/Total Time: 20 min.

Danielle Weets, Grandview, Washington

I created this fresh-tasting side when I tried making a pasta salad I enjoyed at a wedding rehearsal. The easy-to-make dish is a frequent request at parties.

- 1 package (19 ounces) frozen cheese tortellini
- 3/4 cup shredded Parmesan cheese
- 1 can (2-1/4 ounces) sliced ripe olives, drained
- 5 bacon strips, cooked and crumbled
- 1/4 cup prepared pesto

Cook tortellini according to package directions; drain and rinse in cold water. Place in a small bowl. Add remaining ingredients; toss to coat. **Yield: 5 servings.**

easter bread

Prep: 25 min. + rising / **Bake:** 30 min. + cooling

Dolores Skrout, Summerhill, Pennsylvania

Both the Italians and the Swiss prepare this festive Easter bread with colored eggs embedded in the dough. It's a "must-have" at our holiday meal and a delicious way to celebrate.

- 3 to 3-1/2 cups all-purpose flour
- 1/4 cup sugar
- 1 package (1/4 ounce) active dry yeast
- 1 teaspoon salt
- 2/3 cup warm milk (120° to 130°)
- 2 tablespoons butter, softened
- 7 eggs
- 1/2 cup chopped mixed candied fruit
- 1/4 cup chopped blanched almonds
- 1/2 teaspoon aniseed
- Canola oil

In a large bowl, combine 1 cup flour, sugar, yeast and salt. Add milk and butter; beat 2 minutes on medium. Add 2 eggs and 1/2 cup flour; beat 2 minutes on high. Stir in fruit, nuts and aniseed; mix well. Stir in enough remaining flour to form a soft dough.

Turn onto a lightly floured surface; knead until smooth and elastic, 6-8 minutes. Place in a greased bowl; turn once to grease top. Cover and let rise in a warm place until doubled, about 1 hour.

If desired, dye remaining eggs (leave them uncooked); lightly rub with oil. Punch dough down. Divide in half; roll each piece into a 24-in. rope. Loosely twist ropes and tuck eggs into openings. Cover and let dough rise until doubled, about 30 minutes.

Bake at 350° for 30-35 minutes or until golden brown. Remove from pan; cool on a wire rack. **Yield: 1 loaf.**

easter bread

fresh mozzarella tomato salad

fresh mozzarella tomato salad

Prep/Total Time: 15 min.

Regina Wood, Mackenzie, British Columbia

It will only take you a few minutes to prepare this attractive salad that is a perfect fit for a special luncheon. Basil is the finishing touch and adds a burst of color.

- 3 medium tomatoes, sliced
- 8 ounces fresh mozzarella cheese, thinly sliced
- 1/4 cup olive oil
- 2 tablespoons minced fresh basil
- 1/4 teaspoon salt
- 1/4 teaspoon coarsely ground pepper

Alternate tomato and cheese slices on a platter. Drizzle with oil; sprinkle with the basil, salt and pepper. Serve immediately. **Yield: 6 servings.**

parmesan red potatoes

Prep: 10 min. / **Cook:** 20 min. + cooling

Coleen Morrissey, Sweet Valley, Pennsylvania

Ever since I bought a pressure cooker, my busy family hasn't had to miss out on otherwise time-consuming suppers. These tender, cheesy potatoes soak up flavor from the chicken broth and seasonings making them absolutely delectable.

- 4 unpeeled medium red potatoes, quartered
- 1/3 cup grated Parmesan cheese
- 3 teaspoons garlic powder
- 1 can (14-1/2 ounces) chicken broth
- 2 tablespoons minced fresh parsley

Place potatoes in a 6-qt. pressure cooker. Sprinkle with cheese and garlic powder; add broth. Close cover securely; place pressure regulator on vent pipe. Bring cooker to full pressure over high heat. Reduce heat to medium-high; cook for 6 minutes. (Pressure regulator should maintain a slow steady rocking motion; adjust heat if needed.)

Remove pressure cooker from the heat; immediately cool according to manufacturer's directions until pressure is completely reduced. Sprinkle with parsley. **Yield: 4 servings.**

Editor's Note: Parmesan Red Potatoes was tested at 13 pounds of pressure (psi).

portobellos parmesano

Prep/Total Time: 25 min.

Taste of Home Test Kitchen

Our home economists came up with this simple-to-fix meatless entree. Shredded fontina cheese and marinara sauce give real Italian flair to this satisfying twist on eggplant Parmesan.

- 2 large portobello mushroom caps (about 4 to 5 inches wide)
- 1 teaspoon olive oil
- 3/4 cup meatless spaghetti sauce, *divided*
- 1/4 cup shredded fontina cheese
- 1 tablespoon shredded Parmesan cheese

Remove and discard stems from mushrooms. Place the mushrooms, cap side up, on a baking sheet coated with cooking spray. Brush tops with oil. Broil 4-6 in. from the heat for 4-5 minutes or until tender.

Spread half of the spaghetti sauce into an 11-in. x 7-in. baking dish coated with cooking spray. Place mushrooms on sauce, cap side down. Sprinkle with cheese. Drizzle with remaining spaghetti sauce. Sprinkle with Parmesan cheese.

Bake, uncovered, at 350° for 8-10 minutes or until heated through. **Yield: 2 servings.**

portobellos parmesano

roasted garlic bread

Prep: 45 min. + rising / **Bake:** 20 min. + cooling

Barb Alexander, Princeton, New Jersey

The wonderful aroma of this bread baking creates such a cozy feeling in the kitchen. Fresh roasted garlic really adds to the appeal of this loaf.

- 2 medium whole garlic bulbs
- 2 teaspoons olive oil
- 1 package (1/4 ounce) active dry yeast
- 1 cup warm water (110° to 115°)
- 1 tablespoon sugar
- 1 teaspoon salt
- 2-1/2 to 3 cups all-purpose flour
- 2 tablespoons minced fresh sage *or* 2 teaspoons rubbed sage
- 2 teaspoons minced fresh marjoram *or* 3/4 teaspoon dried marjoram
- 1 teaspoon minced fresh rosemary *or* 1/2 teaspoon dried rosemary, crushed
- 2 tablespoons grated Parmesan cheese
- 1 tablespoon butter, melted

Remove papery outer skin from garlic (do not peel or separate cloves). Cut top off garlic bulbs; brush with oil. Wrap each bulb in heavy-duty foil. Bake at 425° for 30-35 minutes or until softened. Cool for 10-15 minutes. Squeeze softened garlic into a small bowl; set aside.

In a large bowl, dissolve the yeast in warm water. Add the sugar, salt and 1 cup flour; beat until smooth. Stir in enough remaining flour to form a soft dough.

Turn onto a lightly floured surface; knead the dough until smooth and elastic, about 6-8 minutes. Place dough in a bowl coated with cooking spray, turning once to coat top. Cover and let rise in a warm place until doubled, about 45 minutes. Meanwhile, add the sage, marjoram and rosemary to the reserved roasted garlic.

Punch dough down. Turn onto a lightly floured surface; divide in half. Roll each portion into a 10-in. x 8-in. rectangle. Spread garlic mixture to within 1/2 in. of edges. Sprinkle with Parmesan cheese. Roll up jelly-roll style, starting with a long side; pinch seam and ends to seal.

Coat a baking sheet with cooking spray. Place loaves seam side down on pan; tuck ends under. With a sharp knife, make several slashes across the top of each loaf. Cover and let rise until doubled, about 30 minutes.

Bake at 375° for 20-25 minutes or until golden brown. Remove the loaves to wire racks; brush loaves with melted butter. **Yield: 2 loaves (10 slices each).**

tuscan bean salad

Prep/Total Time: 30 min.

Cori Rothe, Livermore, California

Enjoy this refreshing medley with a panini or wrap. It's a "can't-miss" side dish that's jam-packed with juicy veggies, wonderful flavor and easy convenience.

- 2 cans (15 ounces *each*) white kidney *or* cannellini beans, rinsed and drained
- 1 jar (6-1/2 ounces) marinated artichoke hearts, undrained
- 1 cup roasted sweet red peppers, cut into 1-inch strips
- 3/4 cup sliced ripe olives
- 1/2 cup chopped red onion
- 1/4 cup oil-packed sun-dried tomatoes, chopped
- 2 tablespoons olive oil
- 2 tablespoons white balsamic vinegar
- 1/4 teaspoon salt
- 1/4 teaspoon pepper
- 1/4 cup fresh basil leaves, thinly sliced

In a large salad bowl, combine the first 10 ingredients. Refrigerate for 20 minutes or until serving. Stir in basil. Serve with a slotted spoon. **Yield: 6 servings.**

Tip! basil basics

To quickly chop a lot of basil with attractive results, stack several basil leaves and roll them into a tight tube. Slice the leaves widthwise into narrow pieces to create long thin strips. If you like smaller pieces, simply chop the strips. This method also works well with other leaf herbs.

super italian chopped salad

Prep/Total Time: 25 min.

Kim Molina, Duarte, California

Traditional antipasto ingredients are sliced and diced to make this substantial salad. I like to buy sliced meat from the deli and chop it all up so you get a bit of everything in each bite.

- 3 cups torn romaine
- 1 can (15 ounces) garbanzo beans *or* chickpeas, rinsed and drained
- 1 jar (6-1/2 ounces) marinated artichoke hearts, drained and chopped
- 1 medium green pepper, chopped
- 2 medium tomatoes, chopped
- 1 can (2-1/4 ounces) sliced ripe olives, drained
- 5 slices deli ham, chopped
- 5 thin slices hard salami, chopped
- 5 slices pepperoni, chopped
- 3 slices provolone cheese, chopped
- 2 green onions, chopped
- 1/4 cup olive oil
- 2 tablespoons red wine vinegar
- 1/4 teaspoon salt
- 1/8 teaspoon pepper
- 2 tablespoons grated Parmesan cheese
- Pepperoncinis, optional

In a large bowl, combine the first 11 ingredients. For the dressing, in a small bowl, whisk the oil, vinegar, salt and pepper. Pour over salad; toss to coat. Sprinkle with cheese. Top with pepperoncinis if desired. **Yield: 10 servings.**

Editor's Note: Look for pepperoncinis (pickled peppers) in the pickle and olive section of your grocery store.

super italian chopped salad

roasted vegetables

Prep/Total Time: 25 min.

Taste of Home Test Kitchen

This tasty medley of oven-baked vegetables is ideal with fish or most any meat. Zucchini and sweet orange bell pepper make its presentation so colorful. I've also found that yellow summer squash or red or green pepper work well.

- 1 medium zucchini, cut into 1/4-inch slices
- 1-1/2 cups sliced baby portobello mushrooms
- 1 medium sweet orange pepper, julienned
- 1 tablespoon olive oil
- 1 tablespoon butter, melted
- 1 teaspoon Italian seasoning
- 1/2 teaspoon salt
- 1/8 teaspoon pepper

In a large bowl, combine the zucchini, mushrooms and orange pepper. Add the remaining ingredients and toss to coat.

Arrange vegetables in a single layer in a 15-in. x 10-in. x 1-in. baking pan coated with cooking spray. Bake, uncovered, at 450° for 15-20 minutes or until tender, stirring occasionally. **Yield: 4 servings.**

marinated pasta salad

Prep: 15 min. + chilling

Gail Buss, Citrus Springs, Maryland

When I have guests coming over or a busy day ahead, I like to make this salad because I prepare it the evening before.

- 1 package (16 ounces) medium pasta shells
- 1/4 pound hard salami, cubed
- 1/4 pound sliced pepperoni, halved
- 1 block (4 ounces) provolone cheese, cubed
- 4 medium tomatoes, seeded and chopped
- 4 celery ribs, chopped
- 1 medium green pepper, chopped
- 1/2 cup sliced pimiento-stuffed olives
- 1/2 cup sliced ripe olives
- 1 bottle (8 ounces) Italian salad dressing
- 2 teaspoons dried oregano
- 1/2 teaspoon pepper

Cook pasta according to package directions; drain pasta and rinse in cold water.

Place in a gallon-size resealable plastic bag; add the salami, pepperoni, cheese, vegetables and olives. Add the salad dressing, oregano and pepper; seal and turn to coat. Cover and refrigerate overnight. Transfer salad to a serving bowl. **Yield: 12-16 servings.**

basil-cheese bread strips

Prep: 15 min. + standing / **Bake:** 15 min.

Melinda Rhoads, Slippery Rock, Pennsylvania

Tender and chewy, these savory breadsticks always go fast thanks to the Italian seasonings and cheese. My daughters could eat every last one.

- 2-1/2 cups all-purpose flour
- 1/4 cup toasted wheat germ
- 1 package (1/4 ounce) active dry yeast
- 1 cup warm water (120° to 130°)
- 2 tablespoons olive oil, *divided*
- 1 tablespoon honey
- 1/2 teaspoon salt
- 2 garlic cloves, minced
- 1/4 cup shredded part-skim mozzarella cheese
- 2 tablespoons grated Parmesan cheese
- 2 tablespoons minced fresh parsley
- 10 fresh basil leaves, coarsely chopped

In a large bowl, combine 1-1/2 cups flour, wheat germ, yeast, water, 1 tablespoon oil, honey and salt; beat for 2 minutes. Stir in enough remaining flour to make a soft dough.

Turn onto a floured surface; knead for 5-6 minutes. Cover and let rest for 10 minutes. Coat a 15-in. x 10-in. x 1-in. baking pan with cooking spray. Pat dough into pan. Bake at 425° for 10 minutes or until golden brown.

In a small bowl, combine garlic and remaining oil; brush over bread. Sprinkle with cheeses, parsley and basil. Bake 5 minutes longer or until cheese is melted. Cut into strips. Refrigerate leftovers. **Yield: 2 dozen.**

tuscan tossed salad

Prep/Total Time: 30 min.

Elaine Sweet, Dallas, Texas

I like to let this appetizing medley sit awhile so the flavors can blend. Serve it in a pretty, clear trifle bowl, and you'll have a stunning side dish on the table.

- 1 loaf (1 pound) focaccia bread, cut into 1-inch cubes
- 1 tablespoon plus 1/4 cup olive oil, *divided*
- 1/2 cup balsamic vinegar
- 1/3 cup minced fresh basil
- 4 anchovy fillets, rinsed and chopped
- 2 garlic cloves, minced
- 1/4 teaspoon salt
- 1/4 teaspoon pepper
- 1 package (5 ounces) spring mix salad greens
- 3 large yellow *or* red tomatoes, seeded and chopped
- 3 cups grape tomatoes
- 2 medium cucumbers, peeled, seeded and diced
- 1/2 cup pitted Greek olives, halved
- 1/2 cup chopped celery
- 1/2 cup chopped red onion
- 1 jar (7 ounces) roasted sweet red peppers, drained and sliced

Place bread cubes in a single layer on a baking sheet; drizzle with 1 tablespoon oil. Bake at 400° for 5-7 minutes or until lightly toasted. Cool on a wire rack.

For the dressing, in a small bowl, whisk the vinegar, basil, anchovies, garlic, salt, pepper and remaining oil. In a large bowl, combine the greens, tomatoes, cucumbers, olives, celery, onion and red peppers.

In a 3-qt. trifle bowl or deep salad bowl, layer a third of the bread cubes and a third of the greens mixture; drizzle with a third of the dressing. Repeat layers twice. Cover salad and refrigerate until serving. **Yield: 16 servings.**

baked pasta

meaty spinach manicotti / page 52

Gooey lasagna...cheesy ziti...hearty stuffed shells... Here we showcase timeless baked entrees, plus a few new twists, too. Baked to bubbly perfection, these dishes capture the essence of home cooking.

broccoli chicken lasagna 42
stuffed shells florentine 42
baked ziti 43
cannelloni 43
chicken spinach manicotti 44
alfredo chicken lasagna 45
fire-roasted ziti with sausage 45
eggplant parmigiana 46
lasagna rolls 46
spaghetti pie 47
overnight spinach manicotti 47
makeover cheese-stuffed shells 48
roasted vegetable lasagna 48
mostaccioli bake 49
italian stuffed shells 49
four-cheese bow ties 50
spinach-stuffed shells 50
sausage broccoli manicotti 51
penne sausage bake 51
meaty spinach manicotti 52
baked mostaccioli 52
spinach and turkey sausage lasagna 53
creamy chicken lasagna 54
italian spaghetti bake 54
turkey manicotti 55
baked ziti with fresh tomatoes 55

broccoli chicken lasagna

broccoli chicken lasagna

Prep: 20 min. / **Bake:** 50 min. + standing

Dawn Owens, Palatka, Florida

As a working mother with four children, I often turn to various pasta dishes for dinner. This lasagna recipe is a little different than the traditional version since it doesn't have tomato sauce—just lots of chicken, ham and cheese.

1/2	pound sliced fresh mushrooms
1	large onion, chopped
1/4	cup butter, cubed
1/2	cup all-purpose flour
1/2	teaspoon salt
1/4	teaspoon pepper
1/8	teaspoon ground nutmeg
1	can (14-1/2 ounces) chicken broth
1-3/4	cups milk
2/3	cup grated Parmesan cheese
1	package (16 ounces) frozen broccoli cuts, thawed
9	lasagna noodles, cooked and drained
1-1/3	cups julienned fully cooked ham, *divided*
2	cups (8 ounces) shredded Monterey Jack cheese, *divided*
2	cups cubed cooked chicken

In a large skillet, saute mushrooms and onion in butter until tender. Stir in the flour, salt, pepper and nutmeg until blended. Gradually stir in broth and milk. Bring to a boil; cook and stir for 2 minutes or until thickened. Stir in Parmesan cheese and broccoli; heat through.

Spread 1/2 cup broccoli mixture in a greased 13-in. x 9-in. baking dish. Layer with three noodles, a third of the remaining broccoli mixture, 1 cup ham and 1 cup Monterey Jack cheese. Top with three noodles, half of the remaining broccoli mixture,

all of the chicken and 1/2 cup Monterey Jack cheese. Top with remaining noodles, broccoli mixture and ham.

Cover and bake at 350° for 45-50 minutes or until bubbly. Sprinkle with remaining shredded Monterey Jack cheese. Bake 5 minutes longer or until cheese is melted. Let stand for 15 minutes before cutting. **Yield: 12 servings.**

stuffed shells florentine

Prep: 15 min. / **Bake:** 30 min.

Trisha Kuster, Macomb, Illinois

For a fancier gathering, I like to serve these pasta shells stuffed with cheese and spinach and topped with spaghetti sauce. The aroma of this entree baking in the oven is so inviting.

1	package (12 ounces) jumbo pasta shells
1	egg, lightly beaten
2	cartons (15 ounces *each*) ricotta cheese
1	package (10 ounces) frozen chopped spinach, thawed and squeezed dry
1/2	cup grated Parmesan cheese
1/2	teaspoon salt
1/2	teaspoon dried oregano
1/4	teaspoon pepper
1	jar (32 ounces) spaghetti sauce
	Thin breadsticks, optional

Cook pasta shells according to package directions. Meanwhile, in a large bowl, combine the egg, ricotta cheese, spinach, Parmesan cheese, salt, oregano and pepper. Drain shells and rinse in cold water; stuff with spinach mixture.

Place shells in a greased 13-in. x 9-in. baking dish. Pour the spaghetti sauce over shells. Cover and bake at 350° for 30-40 minutes or until heated through. Serve with breadsticks if desired. **Yield: 8-10 servings.**

stuffed shells florentine

baked ziti

Prep: 20 min. / **Bake:** 50 min.

Charity Burkholder, Pittsboro, Indiana

My children have frowned upon most of my casseroles, but they'll gobble up this cheesy pasta bake anytime. I've tried to include more meatless meals into our menus, and this is one I know I can rely upon. Even the leftovers are well-liked.

3 cups uncooked ziti *or* small tube pasta
1-3/4 cups meatless spaghetti sauce, *divided*
1 cup (8 ounces) 4% cottage cheese
1-1/2 cups (6 ounces) shredded part-skim mozzarella cheese, *divided*
1 egg, lightly beaten
2 teaspoons dried parsley flakes
1/2 teaspoon dried oregano
1/4 teaspoon garlic powder
1/8 teaspoon pepper

Cook pasta according to package directions. Meanwhile, in a large bowl, combine 3/4 cup spaghetti sauce, cottage cheese, 1 cup mozzarella cheese, egg, parsley, oregano, garlic powder and pepper. Drain pasta; stir into cheese mixture.

In a greased 8-in. square baking dish, spread 1/4 cup meatless spaghetti sauce. Top with pasta mixture, remaining sauce and mozzarella cheese.

Cover and bake at 375° for 45 minutes. Uncover; bake 5-10 minutes longer or until bubbly. **Yield: 6 servings.**

cannelloni

Prep: 30 min. / **Bake:** 20 min.

Susan Longyear, Washington, Virginia

Two varieties of sauces—one that's cream-based and one that's tomato-based—make this satisfying dish doubly delicious!

FILLING:

1 large onion, finely chopped
2 tablespoons olive oil
1 garlic clove, minced
1 package (10 ounces) frozen chopped spinach, thawed and squeezed dry
1 pound ground beef
1/4 cup grated Parmesan cheese
2 tablespoons heavy whipping cream
2 eggs, lightly beaten
1/2 teaspoon dried oregano
1 teaspoon salt
1/4 teaspoon pepper
10 lasagna noodles
1 can (24 ounces) tomato sauce, *divided*

CREAM SAUCE:

6 tablespoons butter
6 tablespoons all-purpose flour
1 cup milk
1 cup heavy whipping cream
Salt and pepper to taste
1/2 cup grated Parmesan cheese

In a large skillet, saute onion in olive oil until tender. Add garlic; cook 1 minute longer. Stir in spinach. Cook about 5 minutes or until all the water has evaporated and spinach starts to stick to the pan, stirring constantly. Transfer spinach mixture to a large bowl.

In the same skillet, brown meat; drain and add to spinach mixture. Stir in the cheese, cream, eggs, oregano, salt and pepper; mix well. Set aside.

Cook lasagna noodles according to package directions; drain. Cut each noodle in half widthwise; spread out noodles side by side on a large piece of foil. Place 1 heaping tablespoon of filling at one end of noodle; roll up. Repeat with remaining noodles and filling.

Pour about 1 cup of tomato sauce in the bottom of a 13-in. x 9-in. baking dish. Place two rolls, seam side down, vertically on both sides of the baking dish. Place remaining rolls in four rows of three rolls each; set aside.

For cream sauce, melt butter in a heavy saucepan over medium heat; stir in flour until smooth; gradually add milk and cream. Bring to a boil, cook and stir for 1 minute or until thickened. Remove from heat; season with salt and pepper. Spread cream sauce over lasagna rolls. Cover with remaining tomato sauce. Sprinkle with cheese.

Bake at 375°, uncovered, for 20-30 minutes or until hot and bubbly. **Yield: 8-10 servings.**

chicken spinach manicotti

Prep: 25 min. **/ Bake:** 50 min.

Melissa Holmquist, Pensacola, Florida

This saucy pasta mainstay is so easy and convenient; it's perfect for entertaining and weeknights alike. The scrumptious filled pasta can be assembled in less than 30 minutes, leaving you plenty of time to tend to other things while it bakes to bubbly perfection.

- 1 package (10 ounces) frozen chopped spinach, thawed, *divided*
- 6 ounces frozen diced cooked chicken breast, thawed
- 3 tablespoons butter
- 3 tablespoons all-purpose flour
- 1 cup chicken broth
- 1/2 cup milk
- 3 cans (8 ounces *each*) tomato sauce
- 1 teaspoon dried basil
- 1 teaspoon dried oregano
- 3/4 teaspoon garlic powder
- 3/4 teaspoon brown sugar
- 6 uncooked manicotti shells
- 1 cup (4 ounces) shredded Monterey Jack cheese

Divide the spinach in half; refrigerate one portion for another use. In a sieve or colander, drain the remaining spinach, squeezing to remove any excess liquid. Pat dry; place in a small bowl. Add the chicken; set aside.

In a large saucepan, melt butter. Stir in flour until smooth; gradually add broth and milk. Bring to a boil; cook and stir for 2 minutes or until thickened. Stir in the tomato sauce, basil, oregano, garlic powder and brown sugar; cook over medium heat for 3-4 minutes or until heated through.

Meanwhile, stuff 1/4 cup chicken mixture into each uncooked manicotti shell. Spread 1/2 cup sauce into a greased 11-in. x 7-in. baking dish. Arrange the manicotti over the sauce; top with remaining sauce.

Cover and bake at 350° for 40-45 minutes or until bubbly. Uncover; sprinkle with cheese. Bake 8-10 minutes longer or until cheese is melted. Let manicotti stand for 5 minutes before serving. **Yield: 3 servings.**

alfredo chicken lasagna

Prep: 25 min. / **Bake:** 40 min. + standing

Bridgette Monaghan, Masonville, Iowa

This elegant lasagna is surprisingly simple, which puts it at the top of my list. I've served it often, and everyone comments on its rich, creamy flavor.

- 6 ounces boneless skinless chicken breast, cut into bite-size pieces
- 1 cup sliced fresh mushrooms
- 2 tablespoons chopped onion
- 1 tablespoon olive oil
- 1 garlic clove, minced
- 1 tablespoon all-purpose flour
- 1 cup Alfredo sauce
- 3/4 cup 2% cottage cheese
- 1/4 cup plus 2 tablespoons shredded Parmesan cheese, *divided*
- 1 egg, lightly beaten
- 1/2 teaspoon Italian seasoning
- 1/2 teaspoon dried parsley flakes
- 4 lasagna noodles, cooked and drained
- 1-1/2 cups (6 ounces) shredded part-skim mozzarella cheese

In a large skillet, saute the chicken, mushrooms and onion in oil until chicken is no longer pink. Add garlic; cook 1 minute longer. Stir in flour until blended; gradually stir in Alfredo sauce. Bring to a boil. Reduce heat; simmer, uncovered, for 5 minutes or until thickened.

In a small bowl, combine the cottage cheese, 1/4 cup Parmesan cheese, egg, Italian seasoning and parsley.

Spread 1/2 cup Alfredo mixture in an 8-in. x 4-in. loaf pan coated with cooking spray. Layer with two noodles (trimmed to fit pan), half of the cottage cheese mixture, 3/4 cup Alfredo mixture and 3/4 cup mozzarella cheese. Sprinkle with the remaining Parmesan cheese. Repeat layers.

Cover and bake at 350° for 30 minutes. Uncover; bake lasagna 10 minutes longer or until bubbly. Let stand for 10 minutes before cutting. **Yield: 3 servings.**

fire-roasted ziti with sausage

Prep/Total Time: 30 min.

Jean Komlos, Plymouth, Michigan

Escape from the ordinary with this satisfying entree. Smoked sausage and fire-roasted spaghetti sauce add nice flavor to this pasta dish. Look for fire-roasted sauce alongside with traditional spaghetti sauces at your grocery store.

- 1 package (8 ounces) ziti *or* small tube pasta
- 1 can (28 ounces) Italian diced tomatoes, undrained
- 1 jar (26 ounces) fire-roasted tomato and garlic spaghetti sauce
- 1 package (16 ounces) smoked sausage, sliced
- 2 cups (8 ounces) shredded part-skim mozzarella cheese, *divided*
- 1 cup (8 ounces) 4% cottage cheese

In a large saucepan, cook ziti pasta according to package directions; drain and return to the pan. Stir in the tomatoes, spaghetti sauce and sausage; heat through.

Stir in 1 cup mozzarella cheese and cottage cheese. Top with remaining mozzarella cheese. Cover and heat over medium heat for 2-5 minutes or until mozzarella cheese is melted. **Yield: 8 servings.**

eggplant parmigiana

Prep: 1-1/4 hours / **Bake:** 35 min.

Valerie Belley, St. Louis, Missouri

This comforting eggplant casserole came from my mom and makes a hearty meatless meal. It's a good way to use up any extra eggplant from your garden. The zesty homemade marinara sauce tastes so good.

- 2 medium eggplant, peeled and cut into 1/2-inch slices
- 2 teaspoons salt
- 2 large onions, chopped
- 2 tablespoons minced fresh basil *or* 2 teaspoons dried basil
- 2 bay leaves
- 1 tablespoon minced fresh oregano *or* 1 teaspoon dried oregano
- 1 tablespoon minced fresh thyme *or* 1 teaspoon dried thyme
- 3 tablespoons olive oil
- 1 can (14-1/2 ounces) diced tomatoes, undrained
- 1 can (12 ounces) tomato paste
- 1 tablespoon honey
- 1-1/2 teaspoons lemon-pepper seasoning
- 4 garlic cloves, minced
- 2 eggs, lightly beaten
- 1/2 teaspoon pepper
- 1-1/2 cups dry bread crumbs
- 1/4 cup butter, *divided*
- 8 cups (32 ounces) shredded part-skim mozzarella cheese
- 1 cup grated Parmesan cheese

Place eggplant in a colander; sprinkle with salt. Let stand for 30 minutes. Meanwhile, in a large skillet, saute the onions, basil, bay leaves, oregano and thyme in oil until onions are tender.

Add the tomatoes, tomato paste, honey and lemon-pepper. Bring to a boil. Reduce heat; cover and simmer for 30 minutes. Add the garlic; simmer 10 minutes longer. Discard the bay leaves.

Rinse eggplant slices; pat dry with paper towels. In a shallow bowl, combine eggs and pepper; place bread crumbs in another shallow bowl. Dip eggplant into eggs, then coat with crumbs. Let stand for 5 minutes.

In a large skillet, cook half of the eggplant in 2 tablespoons butter for 3 minutes on each side or until lightly browned. Repeat with remaining eggplant and butter.

In each of two greased 11-in. x 7-in. baking dishes, layer half of each of the eggplant, tomato sauce and mozzarella cheese. Repeat layers. Sprinkle with Parmesan cheese. Bake, uncovered, at 375° for 35 minutes or until bubbly. **Yield: 10-12 servings.**

lasagna rolls

Prep: 25 min. / **Bake:** 10 min.

Mary Lee Thomas, Logansport, Indiana

Folks can't believe these flavor-filled rolls require just five ingredients. Using prepared spaghetti sauce saves me lots of cooking time. My brood never complains when these appear on the table.

- 6 lasagna noodles
- 1 pound ground beef
- 1 jar (15-1/2 ounces) spaghetti sauce
- 1 teaspoon fennel seed, optional
- 2 cups (8 ounces) shredded part-skim mozzarella cheese, *divided*

Cook lasagna noodles according to package directions. Meanwhile, in a large skillet, cook beef over medium heat until no longer pink; drain. Stir in spaghetti sauce and fennel seed if desired; heat through.

Drain noodles. Spread 1/4 cup meat sauce over each noodle; sprinkle with 2 tablespoons cheese. Carefully roll up noodles and place seam side down in an 8-in. square baking dish. Top with remaining sauce and cheese.

Bake, uncovered, at 400° for 10-15 minutes or until heated through and cheese is melted. **Yield: 6 servings.**

spaghetti pie

spaghetti pie

Prep: 25 min. / **Bake:** 25 min.

Ellen Thompson, Springfield, Ohio

A classic Italian combination is remade into a creamy, family-pleasing casserole. This treasured recipe was given to me several years ago, and my gang never seems to grow tired of eating it.

1	pound lean ground beef (90% lean)
1/2	cup finely chopped onion
1/4	cup chopped green pepper
1	cup canned diced tomatoes, undrained
1	can (6 ounces) tomato paste
1	teaspoon dried oregano
3/4	teaspoon salt
1/2	teaspoon garlic powder
1/4	teaspoon sugar
1/4	teaspoon pepper
6	ounces spaghetti, cooked and drained
1	tablespoon butter, melted
2	egg whites, lightly beaten
1/4	cup grated Parmesan cheese
1	cup (8 ounces) fat-free cottage cheese
1/2	cup shredded part-skim mozzarella cheese

In a nonstick skillet, cook the beef, onion and green pepper over medium heat until meat is no longer pink; drain. Stir in the tomatoes, tomato paste, oregano, salt, garlic powder, sugar and pepper; set aside.

In a large bowl, combine the spaghetti, butter, egg whites and Parmesan cheese. Press onto the bottom and up the sides of a 9-in. deep-dish pie plate coated with cooking spray. Top with cottage cheese and beef mixture.

Bake, uncovered, at 350° for 20 minutes. Sprinkle with mozzarella cheese. Bake 5-10 minutes longer or until cheese is melted and filling is heated through. Let stand for 5 minutes before cutting. **Yield: 6 servings.**

overnight spinach manicotti

Prep: 10 min. + chilling / **Bake:** 40 min.

Tonya Fitzgerald, West Monroe, Louisiana

A friend gave me an awesome recipe for manicotti...and I set out to make it a little healthier. Now, whether we're entertaining guests or enjoying a weeknight meal, my husband asks me to serve this. Even kids love it!

1	carton (15 ounces) reduced-fat ricotta cheese
1	package (10 ounces) frozen chopped spinach, thawed and squeezed dry
1-1/2	cups (6 ounces) shredded part-skim mozzarella cheese, *divided*
1/2	cup grated Parmesan cheese, *divided*
2	egg whites
2	teaspoons minced fresh parsley
1/2	teaspoon salt
1/2	teaspoon onion powder
1/2	teaspoon pepper
1/4	teaspoon garlic powder
4-1/2	cups meatless spaghetti sauce
3/4	cup water
1	package (8 ounces) manicotti shells

In a large bowl, combine the ricotta cheese, spinach, 1 cup mozzarella cheese, 1/4 cup Parmesan cheese, egg whites, parsley, salt, onion powder, pepper and garlic powder. Combine spaghetti sauce and water; spread 1 cup in an ungreased 13-in. x 9-in. baking dish. Stuff uncooked manicotti shells with ricotta mixture; arrange over tomato sauce. Top with remaining sauce. Cover and refrigerate overnight.

Remove from the refrigerator 30 minutes before baking. Sprinkle with remaining mozzarella and Parmesan cheeses. Bake, uncovered, at 350° for 40-45 minutes or until heated through. **Yield: 7 servings.**

overnight spinach manicotti

makeover cheese-stuffed shells

Prep: 35 min. / **Bake:** 50 min.

Beth Fleming, Downers Grove, Illinois

You won't believe the mouthwatering flavor in these enticing shells. The home economists made them over without using any reduced-fat ingredients, yet still saved on fat and calories!

3/4	pound lean ground beef (90% lean)
1	Italian turkey sausage link (4 ounces), casing removed
1	large onion, chopped
1	package (10 ounces) frozen chopped spinach, thawed and squeezed dry
1	cup ricotta cheese
1	egg, lightly beaten
1-1/2	cups (6 ounces) shredded part-skim mozzarella cheese, *divided*
1-1/2	cups 4% cottage cheese
1	cup grated Parmesan cheese
1	cup (4 ounces) shredded sharp cheddar cheese
1	teaspoon Italian seasoning
1/4	teaspoon pepper
1/8	teaspoon ground cinnamon, optional
24	jumbo pasta shells, cooked and drained

SAUCE:

3	cans (8 ounces *each*) no-salt-added tomato sauce
1	tablespoon dried minced onion
1-1/2	teaspoons dried basil
1-1/2	teaspoons dried parsley flakes
2	garlic cloves, minced
1	teaspoon sugar
1	teaspoon dried oregano
1/4	teaspoon pepper

Crumble beef and sausage into a large nonstick skillet; add onion. Cook and stir over medium heat until meat is no longer pink; drain.

Transfer to a large bowl. Stir in the spinach, ricotta and egg. Add 1 cup mozzarella cheese, cottage cheese, Parmesan cheese, shredded sharp cheddar cheese, Italian seasoning, pepper and cinnamon if desired; mix well.

Stuff pasta shells with meat mixture. Arrange in two 11-in. x 7-in. baking dishes coated with cooking spray. Combine the sauce ingredients; spoon over shells.

Cover and bake at 350° for 45 minutes. Uncover; sprinkle with remaining mozzarella cheese. Bake 5-10 minutes longer or until bubbly and cheese is melted. Let stand for 5 minutes before serving. **Yield: 12 servings.**

roasted vegetable lasagna

Prep: 50 min. / **Bake:** 30 min. + standing

Margaret Welder, Madrid, Iowa

With a vegetarian on my guest list, I was inspired to make this lasagna for a party. The bubbly cheese and aroma of roasted veggies make it a dish you can't wait to dig into. Everyone went home with the recipe.

1	small eggplant
2	small zucchini
5	plum tomatoes, seeded
1	large sweet red pepper
1	large onion, cut into small wedges
1/4	cup olive oil
3	tablespoons minced fresh basil, *divided*
3	garlic cloves, minced
3/4	teaspoon salt, *divided*
1/2	teaspoon pepper, *divided*
2/3	cup pitted Greek olives, chopped
1/4	cup butter, cubed
1/4	cup all-purpose flour
2-3/4	cups milk

- 1 bay leaf
- 1/8 teaspoon ground nutmeg
- 5 tablespoons grated Parmesan cheese, *divided*
- 2 tablespoons shredded Asiago cheese
- 3/4 cup shredded part-skim mozzarella cheese
- 6 no-cook lasagna noodles

Cut eggplant, zucchini, tomatoes and red pepper into 1-in. pieces; place in a large bowl. Add onion, oil, 2 tablespoons basil, garlic, 1/2 teaspoon salt and 1/4 teaspoon pepper; toss. Transfer to two greased 15-in. x 10-in. x 1-in. baking pans. Bake at 450° for 20-25 minutes or until crisp-tender. Stir in olives.

In a large saucepan, melt butter; stir in flour until smooth. Gradually stir in milk. Add bay leaf and nutmeg. Bring to a boil; cook and stir for 2 minutes or until thickened. Remove from heat. Stir in 3 tablespoons Parmesan, shredded Asiago and remaining basil, salt and pepper. Discard bay leaf.

Spread a fourth of the sauce in a greased 11-in. x 7-in. baking dish. Top with 2-1/3 cups vegetables, 1/4 cup mozzarella and three noodles. Repeat layers. Top with a fourth of the sauce, remaining vegetables, mozzarella, sauce and Parmesan. Cover and bake at 375° for 30-40 minutes or until bubbly. Let stand 15 minutes before serving. **Yield: 8 servings.**

mostaccioli bake

mixture, remaining pasta mixture and remaining spaghetti sauce. Cover and bake at 350° for 35-40 minutes or until bubbly. Uncover; sprinkle with remaining mozzarella and Parmesan cheeses. Bake 5 minutes longer or until cheese is melted. **Yield: 8 servings.**

mostaccioli bake

Prep: 15 min. / **Bake:** 40 min.

Dorothy Bateman, Carver, Massachusetts

This homey lasagna-style casserole will appeal to the whole family. There's plenty of spaghetti sauce to keep the succulent layers nice and moist.

- 8 ounces uncooked mostaccioli
- 1 egg
- 1 egg white
- 2 cups (16 ounces) 1% cottage cheese
- 1 package (10 ounces) frozen chopped spinach, thawed and squeezed dry
- 1 cup (4 ounces) shredded part-skim mozzarella cheese, *divided*
- 2/3 cup shredded Parmesan cheese, *divided*
- 1/3 cup minced fresh parsley
- 1/4 teaspoon salt
- 1/4 teaspoon pepper
- 2-1/2 cups meatless spaghetti sauce, *divided*

Cook pasta according to package directions. Meanwhile, in a large bowl, combine the egg, egg white, cottage cheese, spinach, 2/3 cup mozzarella cheese, 1/3 cup Parmesan cheese, parsley, salt and pepper; set aside. Drain pasta; stir in 2 cups spaghetti sauce.

Layer half of the pasta mixture in a greased 11-in. x 7-in. baking dish coated with cooking spray. Top with spinach

italian stuffed shells

Prep: 50 min. / **Bake:** 35 min.

Beverly Austin, Fulton, Missouri

A friend shared this hearty entree with me. The cheesy, baked stuffed shells are such a nice change of pace compared to the usual lasagna or spaghetti dish. They're also great for potlucks.

- 1 pound ground beef
- 1 cup chopped onion
- 1 garlic clove, minced
- 2 cups hot water
- 1 can (12 ounces) tomato paste
- 1 tablespoon beef bouillon granules
- 1-1/2 teaspoons dried oregano
- 1 egg, lightly beaten
- 2 cups (16 ounces each) 4% cottage cheese
- 2 cups (8 ounces) shredded part-skim mozzarella cheese, *divided*
- 1/2 cup grated Parmesan cheese
- 24 jumbo shell noodles, cooked and drained

In a large skillet, cook beef, onion and garlic over medium heat until meat is no longer pink; drain. Stir in the water, tomato paste, bouillon and oregano; simmer, uncovered, for 30 minutes.

Meanwhile, in a large bowl, combine the egg, cottage cheese, 1 cup mozzarella and Parmesan cheese. Stuff shells with cheese mixture.

Arrange in a greased 3-qt. baking dish. Pour meat sauce over shells. Cover and bake at 350° for 30 minutes. Uncover; sprinkle with remaining mozzarella cheese. Bake 5 minutes longer or until cheese is melted. **Yield: 6-8 servings.**

four-cheese bow ties

Prep: 20 min. / **Bake:** 30 min.

Mary Farney, Normal, Illinois

With bright red tomatoes and green parsley, this side always looks beautiful when placed on the table in a large serving bowl. My daughter-in-law shared this recipe that's a favorite with her family, and now it's a favorite with ours, too.

1	package (16 ounces) bow tie pasta
2	cans (14-1/2 ounces *each*) diced tomatoes
1/4	cup butter, cubed
1/4	cup all-purpose flour
1/4	teaspoon salt
1/4	teaspoon pepper
1-1/2	cups milk
1-1/2	cups (6 ounces) shredded part-skim mozzarella cheese
1-1/3	cups grated Romano cheese
1/2	cup shredded Parmesan cheese
1/4	cup crumbled blue cheese
1/2	cup minced fresh parsley

Cook pasta according to package directions. Meanwhile, drain tomatoes, reserving 1-1/4 cups juice; set aside.

In a large saucepan, melt butter over medium heat. Stir in the flour, salt and pepper until smooth; gradually add milk and reserved tomato juice. Bring to a boil. Cook and stir for 2 minutes or until thickened. Remove from the heat.

Drain pasta; add the sauce and reserved tomatoes. Stir in cheeses and parsley. Transfer to a greased 3-qt. baking dish (dish will be full). Bake, uncovered, at 375° for 30-35 minutes or until bubbly. **Yield: 12 servings.**

four-cheese bow ties

spinach-stuffed shells

Prep: 25 min. / **Bake:** 25 min.

Debbie Herbert, Seymour, Indiana

Here's a creamy and delicious vegetarian main dish. It comes together in a snap, but looks like you really fussed. I usually serve it with a leafy green salad, freshly baked garlic bread and iced tea.

15	uncooked jumbo pasta shells
1	envelope white sauce mix
1	cup (8 ounces) 4% cottage cheese
1/2	cup shredded part-skim mozzarella cheese
1	egg white
1/2	teaspoon dried basil
1/4	teaspoon garlic powder
Dash pepper	
1	package (10 ounces) frozen chopped spinach, thawed and squeezed dry
1	tablespoon shredded Parmesan cheese

Cook the pasta according to package directions. Meanwhile, prepare the white sauce according to the package directions; set aside.

In a small bowl, combine the cottage cheese, mozzarella cheese, egg white, basil, garlic powder, pepper and half of the spinach (save remaining spinach for another use). Pour half of the white sauce into a greased 11-in. x 7-in. baking dish.

Drain pasta and rinse in cold water; stuff each shell with 2 tablespoons spinach mixture. Arrange over the white sauce. Top with remaining white sauce.

Cover and bake at 375° for 25 minutes or until heated through. Sprinkle with Parmesan cheese. **Yield: 5 servings.**

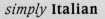

sausage broccoli manicotti

Prep: 25 min. / **Bake:** 40 min.

Jason Jost, Manitowoc, Wisconsin

Even kids will gobble up their broccoli when it's prepared this way. I dress up spaghetti sauce with hearty Italian sausage and garlic, then drizzle it over shells stuffed with broccoli and two cheeses. My wife and daughter love it!

- 1 package (8 ounces) manicotti shells
- 2 cups (16 ounces) 4% cottage cheese
- 3 cups frozen chopped broccoli, thawed and well drained
- 1-1/2 cups (6 ounces) shredded part-skim mozzarella cheese, *divided*
- 3/4 cup shredded Parmesan cheese, *divided*
- 1 egg
- 2 teaspoons minced fresh parsley
- 1/2 teaspoon onion powder
- 1/2 teaspoon pepper
- 1/8 teaspoon garlic powder
- 1 pound bulk Italian sausage
- 4 cups meatless spaghetti sauce
- 2 garlic cloves, minced

Cook manicotti according to package directions. Meanwhile, in a large bowl, combine the cottage cheese, broccoli, 1 cup mozzarella cheese, 1/4 cup Parmesan cheese, egg, parsley, onion powder, pepper and garlic powder; set aside.

In a large skillet, cook the sausage over medium heat until no longer pink; drain. Add spaghetti sauce and garlic. Spread 1 cup meat sauce in a greased 13-in. x 9-in. baking dish.

Rinse and drain shells; stuff with broccoli mixture. Arrange over the sauce. Top with the remaining sauce. Sprinkle with remaining cheeses. Bake, uncovered, at 350° for 40-50 minutes. **Yield: 6-8 servings.**

sausage broccoli manicotti

penne sausage bake

penne sausage bake

Prep: 15 min. / **Bake:** 20 min.

Vicky Benscoter, Birmingham, Alabama

A remarkable dish that is served at our favorite Italian restaurant was the inspiration behind this recipe. You'll find me making the mouthwatering bake frequently for supper since it's simple, yet robust enough for all of us.

- 1 package (16 ounces) uncooked penne pasta
- 1 medium green pepper, chopped
- 1 small onion, chopped
- 1 tablespoon olive oil
- 1 pound Italian turkey sausage links, casings removed
- 3 cups fat-free meatless spaghetti sauce
- 1-1/2 cups (6 ounces) shredded part-skim mozzarella cheese
- 1/4 cup grated Parmesan cheese

Cook pasta according to package directions; drain. In a large skillet, saute green pepper and onion in oil for 6-7 minutes. Add sausage; cook and stir until sausage is no longer pink. Drain. Stir in the spaghetti sauce and pasta.

Transfer to a 3-qt. baking dish coated with cooking spray. Cover and bake at 350° for 15-20 minutes. Uncover; sprinkle with cheeses. Bake 5-10 minutes longer or until cheese is melted. **Yield: 9 servings.**

meaty spinach manicotti

meaty spinach manicotti

Prep: 30 min. / **Bake:** 45 min.

Pat Schroeder, Elkhorn, Wisconsin

My hearty stuffed pasta will feed a crowd. Tangy tomato sauce tops tender manicotti that's filled with a mouthwatering blend of Italian sausage, chicken, spinach and mozzarella cheese. Be prepared to share the recipe!

2	packages (8 ounces *each*) manicotti shells
1/4	cup butter, cubed
1/4	cup all-purpose flour
2-1/2	cups milk
3/4	cup grated Parmesan cheese
1	pound bulk Italian sausage
4	cups cubed cooked chicken *or* turkey
2	packages (10 ounces *each*) frozen chopped spinach, thawed and squeezed dry
2	eggs, lightly beaten
1	cup (4 ounces) shredded part-skim mozzarella cheese
2	jars (26 ounces *each*) spaghetti sauce
1/4	cup minced fresh parsley

Cook manicotti according to package directions. Meanwhile, melt butter in a saucepan. Stir in the flour until smooth; gradually add milk. Bring to a boil; cook and stir for 2 minutes or until thickened. Stir in Parmesan cheese until melted; set aside. Drain manicotti; set aside.

In a large skillet, cook sausage over medium heat until no longer pink; drain. Add the chicken, spinach, eggs, mozzarella cheese and 3/4 cup white sauce. Stuff into manicotti shells.

Spread 1/2 cup spaghetti sauce in each of two ungreased 13-in. x 9-in. baking dishes. Top with manicotti. Pour remaining spaghetti sauce over the top.

Reheat the remaining white sauce, stirring constantly. Pour over spaghetti sauce. Bake, uncovered, at 350° for 45-50 minutes. Sprinkle with parsley. **Yield: 14-16 servings.**

baked mostaccioli

Prep: 35 min. / **Bake:** 30 min.

Darlene Carlson, Jamestown, North Dakota

I came across this recipe several years ago, and it has been a hit with my family ever since. My children especially enjoy the noodles! It's ideal for church potlucks and other gatherings because it serves a large group.

8	ounces uncooked mostaccioli
1-1/2	pounds ground beef
1/2	cup chopped onion
1	garlic clove, minced
1	can (28 ounces) diced tomatoes
1	can (8 ounces) tomato sauce
1	can (6 ounces) tomato paste
1	can (4 ounces) sliced mushrooms
1/2	cup water
1	to 1-1/4 teaspoons salt
1	teaspoon sugar
1	teaspoon dried basil
1/8	teaspoon pepper
1	bay leaf
2	cups (8 ounces) shredded part-skim mozzarella cheese
1/2	cup grated Parmesan cheese

baked mostaccioli

Cook mostaccioli according to package directions; drain and set aside. In a large saucepan, cook beef and onion over medium heat until no longer pink. Add garlic; cook 1 minute longer. Drain.

Stir in the tomatoes, tomato sauce and paste, mushrooms, water, salt, sugar, basil, pepper and bay leaf. Bring to a boil. Reduce heat; simmer, uncovered, for 30 minutes, stirring occasionally.

Discard bay leaf. Stir in mostaccioli. Spoon half into a 13-in. x 9-in. baking dish. Sprinkle with mozzarella cheese; layer with remaining meat mixture. Sprinkle with Parmesan cheese.

Cover and bake at 350 ° for 30-35 minutes or until heated through. Let mostaccioli stand for 5 minutes before serving. **Yield: 10-12 servings.**

spinach and turkey sausage lasagna

Prep: 1 hour / **Bake:** 55 min. + standing

Lynette Randleman, Buffalo, Wyoming

My sausage lasagna proves you can layer on great taste while keeping a luscious comfort food light. My husband prefers this version to the traditional tomato-based recipe.

3	tablespoons butter
1/3	cup all-purpose flour
1/2	teaspoon salt
1/4	teaspoon pepper
3	cups fat-free milk
3	ounces reduced-fat cream cheese, cubed
3/4	cup grated Parmesan cheese
1	pound Italian turkey sausage links, casings removed and crumbled
1	medium onion, chopped
4	garlic cloves, minced
1	teaspoon dried oregano
1	teaspoon dried marjoram
1/2	teaspoon fennel seed, crushed
1	jar (7 ounces) roasted sweet red peppers, drained and chopped
1/2	cup white wine *or* reduced-sodium chicken broth
2	packages (10 ounces *each*) frozen chopped spinach, thawed and squeezed dry
3/4	cup 2% cottage cheese
1/4	teaspoon ground nutmeg
9	lasagna noodles, cooked, rinsed and drained
1/2	cup shredded part-skim mozzarella cheese

In a saucepan, melt butter. Stir in flour, salt and pepper until smooth; gradually stir in milk. Bring to a boil; cook and stir for 1-2 minutes or until thickened. Stir in cream cheese until melted. Stir in Parmesan cheese just until melted. Remove from the heat; set aside.

spinach and turkey sausage lasagna

In a large nonstick skillet coated with cooking spray, cook sausage and onion over medium heat until sausage is no longer pink. Add the garlic, oregano, marjoram and fennel; cook 1 minute longer.

Add roasted peppers and wine. Bring to a boil. Reduce heat; simmer, uncovered, for 3-5 minutes or until liquid is reduced to 3 tablespoons. Remove from the heat; set aside.

In a small bowl, combine the spinach, cottage cheese and nutmeg. Spread 1/2 cup cheese sauce in a 13-in. x 9-in. baking dish coated with cooking spray. Top sauce with three noodles, half of the sausage mixture, half of the spinach mixture and 1 cup sauce; repeat layers. Top with remaining noodles and sauce. Sprinkle with mozzarella cheese.

Cover and bake at 375° for 40 minutes. Uncover; bake 15-20 minutes longer or until heated through and top is lightly browned. Let stand for 10 minutes before cutting. **Yield: 12 servings.**

no-fuss lasagna

When preparing a pan of lasagna, avoid the mess by placing the cheese mixture in a large resealable plastic bag with one corner snipped off. Then, simply squeeze the mixture out evenly onto the noodles. It's easy, cleanup is a breeze and there's no big clumps of cheese.

creamy chicken lasagna

Layer four noodles and half of the chicken mixture in baking dish. Repeat layers. Top with remaining noodles; spread with reserved sauce. Sprinkle with cheddar cheese and paprika.

Cover and bake at 350° for 45-50 minutes or until bubbly. Let stand for 15 minutes before cutting. Sprinkle with parsley. **Yield: 9-12 servings.**

italian spaghetti bake

Prep: 20 min. / Bake: 20 min.

Janice Fredrickson, Elgin, Texas

This hearty recipe makes two large casseroles. The tasty layers of meat sauce, spaghetti and gooey cheese are sure to appeal to pizza-loving kids...and adults. You'll bring home empty pans when you take this to a potluck.

2	packages (one 16 ounces, one 8 ounces) spaghetti
1-1/2	pounds ground beef
1	large green pepper, chopped
1	medium onion, chopped
2	cans (15 ounces *each*) tomato sauce
1	package (8 ounces) sliced pepperoni
1	can (8 ounces) mushroom stems and pieces, drained
1	can (3.8 ounces) sliced ripe olives, drained
1/2	teaspoon dried basil
1/2	teaspoon dried oregano
1/4	teaspoon garlic salt
1/4	teaspoon pepper
4	cups (16 ounces) shredded part-skim mozzarella cheese
1/2	cup grated Parmesan cheese

italian spaghetti bake

creamy chicken lasagna

Prep: 40 min. / Bake: 45 min. + standing

Janice Christofferson, Eagle River, Wisconsin

As a girl, I spent summers on my grandparents' farm and helped harvest bushels of fresh vegetables. To this day, I enjoy making recipes like this lasagna, laden with juicy tomatoes and herbs from my own garden.

12	uncooked lasagna noodles
2	tablespoons cornstarch
1	can (12 ounces) evaporated milk
2	cups chicken broth
1	can (8 ounces) tomato sauce
1/2	cup grated Parmesan cheese
2	garlic cloves, minced
2	teaspoons Dijon mustard
1/2	teaspoon dried basil
1/4	teaspoon ground nutmeg
1/8	teaspoon cayenne pepper
2	cups cooked chicken strips (12 ounces)
24	cherry tomatoes, thinly sliced
1	cup (4 ounces) shredded cheddar cheese
Paprika and minced fresh parsley	

Cook noodles according to package directions. Meanwhile, in a large saucepan, combine cornstarch and milk until smooth. Whisk in the broth, tomato sauce, Parmesan cheese, garlic, mustard, basil, nutmeg and cayenne. Bring to a boil over medium heat; cook and stir for 2 minutes or until thickened. Remove from the heat.

Drain noodles. Spread 1/4 cup sauce into a greased 13-in. x 9-in. baking dish. Set aside 1 cup sauce. Stir chicken and tomatoes into the remaining sauce.

Cook spaghetti according to package directions. Meanwhile, in a Dutch oven, cook the beef, green pepper and onion over medium heat until meat is no longer pink; drain. Stir in the tomato sauce, pepperoni, mushrooms, olives and seasonings. Drain spaghetti.

Spoon 1 cup meat mixture into each of two greased 13-in. x 9-in. baking dishes. Layer with spaghetti and remaining meat mixture. Sprinkle with cheeses.

Cover and freeze one casserole for up to 3 months. Bake the remaining casserole, uncovered, at 350° for 20-25 minutes or until heated through.

To use frozen casserole: Thaw in the refrigerator overnight. Remove from the refrigerator 30 minutes before baking. Cover and bake at 350° for 40 minutes. Uncover; bake 5-10 minutes longer or until cheese is melted. **Yield: 2 casseroles (8 servings each).**

turkey manicotti

Prep: 15 min. + standing / **Bake:** 1 hour 20 min.

Mary Gunderson, Conrad, Iowa

The addition of wholesome bulgur gives extra nutrition to this Italian entree. The pasta is so zesty and flavorful that your family will never realize it's good for them, too.

1/4	cup bulgur
2/3	cup boiling water
3/4	pound lean ground turkey
1-1/2	cups (12 ounces) 2% cottage cheese
1	teaspoon dried basil
1	teaspoon dried oregano
1/2	teaspoon salt
1/4	teaspoon pepper
14	uncooked manicotti shells
1	jar (28 ounces) meatless spaghetti sauce
1/2	cup water
1	cup (4 ounces) shredded part-skim mozzarella cheese

Place the bulgur in a large bowl; stir in boiling water. Cover and let stand for 30 minutes or until the liquid is absorbed. Drain and squeeze dry.

In a nonstick skillet, cook turkey over medium heat until no longer pink; drain. Add the cottage cheese, basil, oregano, salt, pepper and bulgur. Stuff into uncooked manicotti shells. Arrange stuffed shells in a 13-in. x 9-in. baking dish coated with cooking spray.

Combine spaghetti sauce and water; pour over shells. Cover and bake at 350° for 1 hour and 15 minutes or until shells are tender and sauce is bubbly. Uncover; sprinkle with mozzarella cheese. Bake 5 minutes longer or until cheese is melted. **Yield: 7 servings.**

baked ziti with fresh tomatoes

baked ziti with fresh tomatoes

Prep: 70 min. / **Bake:** 30 min.

Barbara Johnson, Decker, Indiana

I prepare the sauce for this filling main dish ahead of time, so it saves precious moments in the evening. The use of fresh tomatoes really adds to its overall flavor!

1	pound ground beef
1	cup chopped onion
3	pounds plum tomatoes, peeled, seeded and chopped (about 15 tomatoes)
1-1/2	teaspoons salt
1	teaspoon dried basil
1/4	teaspoon pepper
8	ounces uncooked ziti
2	cups (8 ounces) shredded part-skim mozzarella cheese, *divided*
2	tablespoons grated Parmesan cheese

In a Dutch oven, cook the beef and onion over medium heat until meat is no longer pink; drain. Stir in the tomatoes, salt, basil and pepper. Reduce heat to low; cover and cook for 45 minutes, stirring occasionally.

Cook ziti according to package directions; drain. Place in a large bowl. Stir in sauce and 1 cup mozzarella cheese. Transfer to a greased 3-qt. baking dish; sprinkle with Parmesan cheese and remaining mozzarella cheese.

Cover and bake at 350° for 15 minutes. Uncover; bake 15 minutes longer or until heated through. **Yield: 6 servings.**

pasta, noodles & sauces

gnocchi in sage butter / page 68

Spaghetti, fettuccine, linguine, rigatoni and penne... these are just some of the pastas featured here. Oodles of noodles, authentic favorites and slowly simmered sauces will have you shouting "Mangia!"

tomato gnocchi with pesto 58
garden primavera fettuccine 58
hearty spaghetti sauce 59
sweet onion 'n' sausage spaghetti 59
tortellini primavera 60
parmesan noodles. 60
ziti with roasted red pepper sauce 61
italian pasta sauce 61
italian spaghetti and meatballs 62
peppy parmesan pasta 62
slow-cooked spaghetti sauce 63
italian sausage with bow ties. 63
artichoke-basil pasta sauce 64
gnocchi chicken skillet. 64
tuxedo pasta 65
fettuccine primavera 66
herbed mushroom spaghetti sauce. 66
blushing penne pasta 67
beef ragu with ravioli. 67
gnocchi in sage butter. 68
chunky pasta sauce 68
alfredo chicken tortellini 69
ravioli skillet. 69
fresh tomato pasta toss. 70
chicken orzo skillet 70
no-cook herbed tomato sauce 71
linguine with fresh tomatoes 71
pasta primavera. 71

tomato gnocchi with pesto

tomato gnocchi with pesto

Prep: 70 min. / **Cook:** 5 min.

Taste of Home Test Kitchen

Our taste panel simply loved the delectable blend of pesto sauce and pine nuts in this elegant and impressive dish created by our home economists. One bite of this authentic entree is worth every minute spent preparing it.

- 1 pound russet potatoes, peeled and quartered
- 3 quarts water
- 2/3 cup all-purpose flour
- 1 egg
- 3 tablespoons tomato paste
- 3/4 teaspoon salt, *divided*

PESTO:
- 2 tablespoons olive oil
- 1 tablespoon water
- 1 cup loosely packed fresh basil
- 1 garlic clove, peeled
- 3 tablespoons grated Parmesan cheese
- 3 tablespoons pine nuts, toasted

Place potatoes in a saucepan and cover with water. Bring to a boil. Reduce heat; cover and simmer for 15-20 minutes or until tender. Drain.

Over warm burner or very low heat, stir the potatoes for 1-2 minutes or until steam is evaporated. Press through a potato ricer or strainer into a small bowl; cool slightly. In a Dutch oven, bring water to a boil.

Using a fork, make a well in the potatoes. Sprinkle flour over potatoes and into well. Whisk the egg, tomato paste and 1/2 teaspoon salt; pour into well. Stir until blended. Knead 10-12 times, forming a soft dough.

Divide dough into four portions. On a floured surface, roll portions into 1/2-in.-thick ropes; cut into 3/4-in. pieces. Press and roll each piece with a lightly floured fork. Cook gnocchi

in boiling water in batches for 30-60 seconds or until they float. Remove with a strainer and keep warm.

For pesto, place the oil, water, basil, garlic and remaining salt in a food processor; cover and process until blended. Stir in Parmesan cheese. Spoon over gnocchi; toss gently to coat. Sprinkle with pine nuts. **Yield: 4 servings.**

garden primavera fettuccine

Prep/Total Time: 30 min.

Tammy Perrault, Lancaster, Ohio

I came up with this recipe while trying to make broccoli Alfredo. I kept adding fresh vegetables, and the result was this creamy and colorful pasta side dish!

- 1 package (12 ounces) fettuccine
- 1 cup fresh cauliflowerets
- 1 cup fresh broccoli florets
- 1/2 cup julienned carrot
- 1 small sweet red pepper, julienned
- 1/2 small yellow summer squash, sliced
- 1/2 small zucchini, sliced
- 1 cup Alfredo sauce
- 1 teaspoon dried basil

Shredded Parmesan cheese, optional

In a large saucepan, cook fettuccine according to package directions, adding vegetables during the last 4 minutes. Drain and return to the pan.

Add Alfredo sauce and basil; toss to coat. Cook over low heat for 1-2 minutes or until heated through. Sprinkle with cheese if desired. **Yield: 10 servings.**

garden primavera fettuccine

hearty spaghetti sauce

hearty spaghetti sauce

Prep: 40 min. / **Cook:** 30 min.

Margaret Malinowski, Queen Creek, Arizona

This chunky old-fashioned sauce will satisfy even the largest appetite. It may look like a lot of work, but it goes together fast and smells so good as it simmers.

8	bacon strips
8	pounds ground beef
4	large onions, chopped
2	large green peppers, diced
1	pound sliced fresh mushrooms
1/2	cup olive oil
16	garlic cloves, minced
1/2	cup all-purpose flour
6	cans (28 ounces *each*) diced tomatoes
2	cans (12 ounces *each*) tomato paste
2	cups water
1	cup white wine vinegar
6	tablespoons sugar
3	tablespoons Worcestershire sauce
2	tablespoons dried celery flakes
2	tablespoons dried oregano
2	tablespoons dried basil
4	teaspoons salt
2	teaspoons celery salt
2	teaspoons cayenne pepper

Hot cooked spaghetti

In a large stockpot, cook bacon over medium heat until crisp. Remove to paper towels to drain. Cook beef over medium heat in drippings until meat is no longer pink; drain. Remove beef and keep warm.

In the same kettle, saute the onions, peppers and mushrooms in oil for 5 minutes or until onions are tender. Add garlic; cook 2 minutes longer.

Stir in the flour until blended. Stir in the diced tomatoes, tomato paste, water, vinegar, sugar, Worcestershire sauce and seasonings. Crumble bacon; return bacon and beef to pan. Bring to a boil. Reduce heat; simmer, uncovered, for 2 hours, stirring occasionally. Serve sauce with spaghetti. **Yield: 38 servings (1 cup each).**

sweet onion 'n' sausage spaghetti

Prep/Total Time: 30 min.

Mary Relyea, Canastota, New York

Sweet onion seasons Italian turkey sausage links and adds robust flavor to this wholesome pasta dish. It takes only minutes to toss together with half-and-half, basil and tomatoes to create this quick, satisfying meal.

6	ounces uncooked whole wheat spaghetti
3/4	pound Italian turkey sausage links, casings removed
2	teaspoons olive oil
1	sweet onion, thinly sliced
1	pint cherry tomatoes, halved
1/2	cup loosely packed fresh basil leaves, thinly sliced
1/2	cup half-and-half cream

Shaved Parmesan cheese, optional

Cook spaghetti according to package directions. Meanwhile, in a large nonstick skillet over medium heat, cook sausage in oil for 5 minutes. Add onion; cook 8-10 minutes longer or until meat is no longer pink and onion is tender.

Stir in tomatoes and basil; heat through. Add cream; bring to a boil. Drain spaghetti; toss with sausage mixture. Garnish with cheese if desired. **Yield: 5 servings.**

sweet onion 'n' sausage spaghetti

tortellini primavera

Prep/Total Time: 20 min.

Mary Ann Dell, Phoenixville, Pennsylvania

This creamy meal-in-one calls for just a few ingredients, such as store-bought pasta, so it's a snap to put together. It's wonderful when zucchini and squash are in great abundance.

- 1 package (9 ounces) refrigerated cheese tortellini
- 2 medium yellow summer squash, chopped
- 2 medium zucchini, chopped
- 2 teaspoons olive oil
- 1 pint cherry tomatoes, halved
- 1/2 cup chopped green onions
- 1/4 teaspoon pepper
- 1/2 cup creamy Caesar salad dressing
- 1/4 cup shredded Parmesan cheese
- 1/4 cup sliced almonds, toasted

Cook tortellini according to package directions.

Meanwhile, in a large skillet, saute the yellow squash and zucchini in olive oil for 4-6 minutes or until the vegetables are crisp-tender.

Drain the tortellini; place tortellini in a large bowl. Add the summer squash and zucchini mixture, cherry tomatoes, chopped green onions and pepper.

Drizzle pasta with Caesar salad dressing; toss to coat. Sprinkle with shredded Parmesan cheese and toasted almonds. **Yield: 6 servings.**

tortellini primavera

parmesan noodles

parmesan noodles

Prep/Total Time: 20 min.

Elizabeth Ewan, Parma, Ohio

The special blend of seasonings and cheese in this saucy dish makes it the perfect companion to any supper. It's a nice change of pace from regular pasta recipes.

- 2 packages (3 ounces *each*) cream cheese, softened
- 1/2 cup butter, softened, *divided*
- 2 tablespoons minced fresh parsley
- 1 teaspoon dried basil
- 1/2 teaspoon lemon-pepper seasoning
- 2/3 cup boiling water
- 1 garlic clove, minced
- 6 cups hot cooked thin noodles
- 2/3 cup grated Parmesan cheese, *divided*
- Additional parsley, optional

In a small bowl, combine the cream cheese, 2 tablespoons butter, parsley, basil and lemon-pepper seasoning. Stir in water; keep warm.

In a saucepan, saute garlic in remaining butter for 1 minute or until golden brown.

Place noodles in a serving bowl; top with garlic mixture. Sprinkle with half of the Parmesan cheese; toss lightly. Spoon cream sauce over noodles and sprinkle with remaining Parmesan cheese. Garnish with parsley if desired. **Yield: 8 servings.**

ziti with roasted red pepper sauce

Prep: 20 min. / **Cook:** 25 min.

Marge Werner, Broken Arrow, Oklahoma

Packed with green beans and gooey, melted cheese, this hearty one-dish meal is one that will satisfy the entire family! Pureed roasted red peppers add zing and color to the sauce.

1	jar (12 ounces) roasted sweet red peppers, drained
1	pound lean ground beef (90% lean)
1	small onion, chopped
1	can (14-1/2 ounces) diced tomatoes, undrained
2	garlic cloves, minced
1	teaspoon dried oregano
1	teaspoon dried basil
3/4	teaspoon salt
8	ounces uncooked ziti *or* small tube pasta
1-1/2	cups cut fresh green beans
1-1/2	cups (6 ounces) shredded part-skim mozzarella cheese

Place peppers in a food processor; cover and process until smooth. In a large skillet, cook beef and onion until meat is no longer pink; drain. Stir in the pepper puree, tomatoes, garlic, oregano, basil and salt. Bring to a boil. Reduce heat; simmer, uncovered, for 15 minutes.

Meanwhile, in a Dutch oven, cook pasta according to package directions, adding green beans during the last 5 minutes of cooking. Cook until pasta and green beans are tender; drain. Return to the pan; stir in meat sauce. Sprinkle with cheese; stir until melted. **Yield: 6 servings.**

ziti with roasted red pepper sauce

italian pasta sauce

italian pasta sauce

Prep: 20 min. / **Cook:** 2 hours

Jeannie Peirce, Brentwood, California

I got this recipe years ago from my boyfriend's Italian barber. I've adjusted it a little, and now it's my specialty. Whip it up for dinner tonight and freeze any remaining sauce to use later.

3	hot Italian sausage links (4 ounces *each*), cut into 1/2-inch slices
1	pound lean ground beef (90% lean)
1	small onion, finely chopped
2	garlic cloves, minced
2	cans (15 ounces *each*) tomato sauce
1	can (14-1/2 ounces) stewed tomatoes
1-2/3	cups crushed tomatoes in puree
1	can (6 ounces) tomato paste
1-1/2	teaspoons sugar
1/8	teaspoon pepper
2	tablespoons minced fresh parsley
1-1/2	teaspoons minced fresh oregano *or* 1/2 teaspoon dried oregano
	Hot cooked pasta

In a large skillet, cook sausage over medium heat until meat is no longer pink; drain. Meanwhile, in a Dutch oven over medium heat, cook beef and onion until meat is no longer pink. Add garlic; cook 1 minute longer. Drain.

Add the tomato sauce, stewed tomatoes, crushed tomatoes, tomato paste, sugar and pepper. Stir in the Italian sausage. Bring to a boil. Reduce heat; cover and simmer for 2 hours, stirring occasionally.

Stir in parsley and oregano. Serve desired amount with pasta. Cool remaining sauce; transfer to freezer containers. Freeze for up to 3 months.

To use frozen sauce: Thaw in the refrigerator overnight. Place in a saucepan and heat through. **Yield: 10 servings.**

italian spaghetti and meatballs

Prep: 30 min. / **Cook:** 1-1/2 hours

Etta Winter, Pavillion, New York

This is an authentic Italian recipe given to me by my cousin's wife. It's so hearty and satisfying, my gang's eyes light up when I tell them that we're having this for supper!

- 2 cans (28 ounces *each*) diced tomatoes, undrained
- 1 can (12 ounces) tomato paste
- 1-1/2 cups water, *divided*
- 3 tablespoons grated onion
- 1 tablespoon sugar
- 1-1/2 teaspoons dried oregano
- 1 bay leaf
- 1-1/4 teaspoons salt, *divided*
- 1 teaspoon minced garlic, *divided*
- 3/4 teaspoon pepper, *divided*
- 6 slices day-old bread, torn into pieces
- 2 eggs, lightly beaten
- 1/2 cup grated Parmesan cheese
- 2 tablespoons minced fresh parsley
- 1 pound ground beef

Hot cooked spaghetti

Additional Parmesan cheese, optional

In a Dutch oven, combine the tomatoes, tomato paste, 1 cup water, onion, sugar, oregano, bay leaf and 1/2 teaspoon each of salt, garlic and pepper. Bring to a boil. Reduce heat and simmer, uncovered, for 1-1/4 hours.

Meanwhile, soak bread in remaining water. Squeeze out excess moisture. In a large bowl, combine the bread, eggs, Parmesan cheese, parsley and remaining salt, garlic and pepper. Crumble beef over mixture and mix well. Shape into thirty-six 1-1/2-in. meatballs.

Place meatballs on a rack in a shallow baking pan. Bake, uncovered, at 400° for 20 minutes or until no longer pink; drain. Transfer to spaghetti sauce. Simmer, uncovered, until heated through, stirring occasionally. Discard bay leaf. Serve with spaghetti with additional Parmesan if desired. **Yield: 6 servings.**

peppy parmesan pasta

Prep/Total Time: 10 min.

Debbie Horst, Phoenix, Arizona

When my husband and I needed an impromptu dinner, we came up with this no-fuss, mouthwatering pasta toss that features delicate angel hair pasta, fresh tomato, pepperoni, ripe olives and Parmesan cheese.

- 8 ounces angel hair pasta
- 1 large tomato, chopped
- 1 package (3 ounces) sliced pepperoni
- 1 can (2-1/4 ounces) sliced ripe olives, drained
- 1/4 cup grated Parmesan cheese
- 3 tablespoons olive oil
- 1/2 teaspoon salt *or* salt-free seasoning blend, optional
- 1/4 teaspoon garlic powder

Cook pasta according to package directions. Meanwhile, in a serving bowl, combine the tomato, pepperoni, olives, cheese, oil, salt if desired and garlic powder. Drain pasta; add to the tomato mixture and toss to coat. **Yield: 4 servings.**

slow-cooked spaghetti sauce

slow-cooked spaghetti sauce

Prep: 15 min. / **Cook:** 6 hours

David Shields, Barberton, Ohio

When I wanted a versatile tomato sauce that could be used for different varieties of dishes, I tried making my own. The result was this thick, meaty sauce that's great not only with spaghetti, but also on pizza.

1	pound ground beef
4	cans (14-1/2 ounces *each*) diced tomatoes, undrained
6	cans (6 ounces *each*) tomato paste
1	cup beef broth
1/4	cup packed brown sugar
3	tablespoons minced fresh marjoram *or* 1 tablespoon dried marjoram
2	tablespoons garlic powder
2	tablespoons minced fresh basil *or* 2 teaspoons dried basil
2	tablespoons minced fresh oregano *or* 2 teaspoons dried oregano
2	tablespoons minced fresh parsley
1	teaspoon salt
1	bay leaf
Hot cooked spaghetti	

In a large skillet, cook beef over medium heat until no longer pink; drain.

Transfer to a 5-qt. slow cooker. Stir in the tomatoes, tomato paste, broth, brown sugar and seasonings. Cover and cook on low for 6-8 hours or until bubbly. Discard bay leaf. Serve with spaghetti. **Yield: 12-14 servings.**

italian sausage with bow ties

Prep/Total Time: 25 min.

Janelle Moore, Federal Way, Washington

Here's a family treasure that's requested monthly in our house. The Italian sausage paired with a creamy tomato sauce is out of this world. This dish is so simple to make, but tastes like you spent hours over a hot stove.

1	package (16 ounces) bow tie pasta
1	pound bulk Italian sausage
1/2	cup chopped onion
1/2	teaspoon crushed red pepper flakes
1-1/2	teaspoons minced garlic
2	cans (14-1/2 ounces *each*) Italian stewed tomatoes, drained and chopped
1-1/2	cups heavy whipping cream
1/2	teaspoon salt
1/4	teaspoon dried basil
Shredded Parmesan cheese	

Cook pasta according to package directions. Meanwhile, in a Dutch oven, cook the sausage, onion and pepper flakes over medium heat for 4-5 minutes or until meat is no longer pink. Add garlic; cook 1 minute longer. Drain.

Stir in the tomatoes, cream, salt and basil. Bring to a boil over medium heat. Reduce heat; simmer, uncovered, for 6-8 minutes or until thickened, stirring occasionally. Drain pasta; toss with sausage mixture. Garnish with cheese. **Yield: 5 servings.**

italian sausage with bow ties

artichoke-basil pasta sauce

Prep: 10 min. **/ Cook:** 10 min.

Janet Bischof, Sumter, South Carolina

I received this recipe from my college roommate, and it quickly became one of my favorites. Fresh basil and minced garlic give the meatless pasta sauce just the right amount of Italian flair, while artichoke hearts make it deliciously different.

- 1 jar (6-1/2 ounces) marinated artichoke hearts
- 1 cup chopped onion
- 1 cup sliced fresh mushrooms
- 1/2 teaspoon minced garlic
- 1 can (14-1/2 ounces) diced tomatoes, undrained
- 1 cup water
- 1 can (6 ounces) tomato paste
- 2 tablespoons minced fresh basil *or* 2 teaspoons dried basil
- 1 teaspoon sugar
- 1/2 teaspoon salt, optional

Hot cooked pasta

Drain the artichoke hearts, reserving the marinade; set the artichokes aside.

In a large saucepan, saute onion and mushrooms in reserved marinade for 2-3 minutes or until tender. Add garlic; cook 1 minute longer.

Stir in the artichokes, diced tomatoes, water, tomato paste, basil, sugar and salt if desired. Bring to a boil.

Reduce heat; simmer, uncovered, for 5-10 minutes or until the sauce is heated through. Serve the sauce over hot cooked pasta. **Yield: 5 servings.**

artichoke-basil pasta sauce

gnocchi chicken skillet

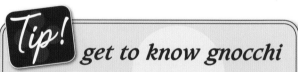

gnocchi chicken skillet

Prep/Total Time: 25 min.

Taste of Home Test Kitchen

In this simple dinner meal, tender gnocchi are draped in a robust, flavorful meat sauce that uses healthy ground chicken.

- 1 package (10 ounces) potato gnocchi
- 1 pound ground chicken
- 1/2 cup chopped onion
- 2 tablespoons olive oil
- 1 jar (26 ounces) spaghetti sauce
- 1/4 to 1/2 teaspoon dried oregano
- 1/4 teaspoon salt

Shredded Parmesan cheese, optional

Prepare gnocchi according to package directions. Meanwhile, in a large skillet, cook chicken and onion in oil over medium heat until chicken is no longer pink. Stir in the sauce, oregano and salt.

Drain gnocchi; add to skillet. Cover; cook 10-15 minutes or until heated through. Serve with cheese if desired. **Yield: 4 servings.**

Tip! *get to know gnocchi*

Gnocchi are Italian dumplings traditionally made with potatoes and flour or farina. Eggs and seasonings are added before the dough is shaped into long ropes, then cut into small pieces and rolled into balls. The balls are rolled over the tines of a fork or a special gnocchi board to make small ridges in the dough that help the gnocchi cook faster and hold onto whatever sauce you choose.

tuxedo pasta

Prep/Total Time: 20 min.

Jackie Hannahs, Fountain, Michigan

With juicy chicken and fresh veggies, this pasta medley tossed in a mild lemon and wine sauce creates a complete, no-fuss meal in minutes. I try to keep leftover chicken or turkey on hand so that I can fix this dish at a moment's notice.

2	cups uncooked bow tie pasta
2	cups cubed cooked chicken
1	medium zucchini, sliced
1-1/2	cups sliced fresh mushrooms
1/2	cup chopped sweet red pepper
3	tablespoons butter, *divided*
1/4	cup lemon juice
2	tablespoons white wine *or* chicken broth
3/4	cup shredded Parmesan cheese
3	tablespoons minced fresh basil *or* 1 tablespoon dried basil

Cook pasta according to package directions. Meanwhile, in a large skillet, saute the chicken, zucchini, mushrooms and red pepper in 2 tablespoons butter for 4-5 minutes or until vegetables are tender. Add the lemon juice and wine. Bring to a boil. Reduce heat; cook and stir for 2 minutes or until heated through.

Drain pasta; add to skillet. Stir in the cheese, basil and remaining butter. **Yield: 6 servings.**

fettuccine primavera

Prep/Total Time: 20 min.

Taste of Home Test Kitchen

For a delicious way to get your family to eat their veggies, try this creamy pasta dish from our home economists. Every bite features a variety of garden-fresh vegetables, juicy chunks of chicken and mouthwatering flavor.

    1   package (16 ounces) fettuccine, cooked
        and drained
    1   cup fresh small broccoli florets
   10   asparagus spears, trimmed and cut into
        1-1/2-inch pieces
    2   tablespoons water
    2   boneless skinless chicken breast halves,
        cut into 1-inch strips
    6   tablespoons butter, *divided*
    1   small zucchini, sliced
    1   cup diagonally sliced carrots
    1   cup sliced mushrooms
    1   cup snow peas
  1/2   cup sweet red pepper strips
  1/2   cup sliced green onions
    1   garlic clove, minced
    2   tablespoons olive oil
Salt and pepper to taste
    2   cups heavy whipping cream
  1/2   cup minced fresh parsley
  1/2   cup shredded Parmesan cheese

In a large saucepan, cook fettuccine according to package directions; drain. Meanwhile, place broccoli and asparagus in a small microwave-safe bowl. Add water; cover and cook on high for 2 minutes. Immediately rinse vegetables with cold water; drain thoroughly. Set aside.

In a large skillet, stir-fry chicken in 2 tablespoons butter for 3 minutes or until no longer pink. Remove the chicken from skillet and set aside.

In the same skillet, cook zucchini, carrots, mushrooms, snow peas, red pepper, green onions and garlic in remaining butter and olive oil until tender. Transfer the vegetables, including the broccoli and asparagus, to a large bowl. Season with salt and pepper.

In the same skillet, bring cream to a boil. Boil for 2-3 minutes, stirring constantly. Add cooked fettuccine and parsley to cream; toss until noodles are coated. Add fettuccine mixture to vegetables. Add chicken and toss to combine. Place on serving platter. Sprinkle with cheese. **Yield: 4 servings.**

herbed mushroom spaghetti sauce

Prep: 15 min. / **Cook:** 45 min.

Anne Halfhill, Sunbury, Ohio

Ground beef makes this rich spaghetti sauce extra hearty. The blend of herbs provides wonderful taste.

    1   pound lean ground beef (90% lean)
  1/2   pound sliced fresh mushrooms
    1   large onion, chopped
    1   small green pepper, chopped
    2   tablespoons olive oil
    4   garlic cloves, minced
    2   cans (8 ounces *each*) tomato sauce
    1   can (10-3/4 ounces) condensed tomato soup,
        undiluted
    1   teaspoon dried basil
  1/2   teaspoon salt, optional
  1/2   teaspoon dried rosemary, crushed
  1/2   teaspoon dried oregano
  1/4   teaspoon pepper
Hot cooked spaghetti

In a large skillet, cook the beef, mushrooms, onion and green pepper in oil over medium heat until meat is no longer pink. Add garlic; cook 1 minute longer. Drain. Stir in the tomato sauce, soup and seasonings. Bring to a boil; reduce heat.

Cover and simmer for 45-60 minutes, stirring occasionally. Serve with spaghetti. **Yield: 6 servings.**

herbed mushroom spaghetti sauce

blushing penne pasta

Prep/Total Time: 30 min.

Margaret Wilson, Sun City, California

I reworked this recipe from the original version, which called for vodka and heavy whipping cream, to a version that uses half-and-half and white wine. My friends and family have a difficult time believing a sauce this scrumptious and smooth could really be light.

1	package (16 ounces) penne pasta
1	cup thinly sliced onions
2	tablespoons butter
2	tablespoons minced fresh thyme *or* 2 teaspoons dried thyme
2	tablespoons minced fresh basil *or* 2 teaspoons dried basil
1	teaspoon salt
1-1/2	cups half-and-half cream, *divided*
1/2	cup white wine *or* reduced-sodium chicken broth
1	tablespoon tomato paste
2	tablespoons all-purpose flour
1/2	cup shredded Parmigiano-Reggiano cheese, *divided*

Cook penne according to package directions. Meanwhile, in a large nonstick skillet over medium heat, cook onions in butter for 8-10 minutes or until lightly browned. Add the thyme, basil and salt; cook 1 minute longer. Add 1 cup cream, wine and tomato paste; cook and stir until blended.

Combine the flour and the remaining cream until smooth; gradually stir into onion mixture. Bring to a boil; cook and stir for 2 minutes or until thickened. Stir in 1/4 cup cheese. Drain penne; toss with sauce. Sprinkle pasta with remaining cheese. **Yield: 8 servings.**

beef ragu with ravioli

Prep: 15 min. / **Cook:** 40 min.

Taste of Home Test Kitchen

This slightly sweet, no-stress sauce from our home economists tastes like it was simmering all day! Serve it over your favorite refrigerated or frozen ravioli for a meal in minutes.

1	pound ground beef
1/2	cup chopped onion
1	pound plum tomatoes, diced
1	cup beef broth
1/2	cup red wine *or* additional beef broth
1	can (6 ounces) tomato paste
2	teaspoons minced fresh rosemary
1	teaspoon sugar
1	teaspoon minced garlic
1/2	teaspoon salt
1	package (20 ounces) refrigerated cheese ravioli

Grated Parmesan cheese, optional

In a large skillet, cook beef and onion over medium heat until meat is no longer pink; drain. Add the tomatoes, broth, wine, tomato paste, rosemary, sugar, garlic and salt. Bring to a boil. Reduce heat; simmer, uncovered, for 30 minutes.

Cook ravioli according to package directions; drain. Serve with meat sauce. Sprinkle with grated Parmesan cheese if desired. **Yield: 4 servings.**

gnocchi in sage butter

Prep: 70 min. / **Cook:** 5 min.

Taste of Home Test Kitchen

A buttery garlic and sage sauce makes these tender, homemade gnocchi simply melt in your mouth. The simplicity of this Italian-inspired meal is one of the reasons our home economists regard this recipe as a treasure.

- 1 pound russet potatoes, peeled and quartered
- 2/3 cup all-purpose flour
- 1 egg
- 1/2 teaspoon salt
- Dash ground nutmeg
- 2 tablespoons butter
- 2 garlic cloves, thinly sliced
- 4 fresh sage leaves, thinly sliced

Place potatoes in a saucepan and cover with water. Bring to a boil. Reduce heat; cover and simmer for 15-20 minutes or until tender. Drain.

Over warm burner or very low heat, stir potatoes for 1-2 minutes or until steam is evaporated. Press through a potato ricer or strainer into a small bowl; cool slightly. In a Dutch oven, bring 3 qts. water to a boil.

Using a fork, make a well in the potatoes. Sprinkle flour over potatoes and into well. Whisk the egg, salt and nutmeg; pour into well. Stir until blended. Knead 10-12 times, forming a soft dough.

Divide dough into four portions. On a floured surface, roll portions into 1/2-in.-thick ropes; cut into 3/4-in. pieces. Press and roll each piece with a lightly floured fork. Cook gnocchi in boiling water in batches for 30-60 seconds or until they float. Remove with a strainer and keep warm.

In a large heavy saucepan, cook butter over medium heat for 3 minutes. Add garlic and sage; cook for 1-2 minutes or until butter and garlic are golden brown. Add gnocchi; stir gently to coat. Serve immediately. **Yield: 4 servings.**

gnocchi in sage butter

chunky pasta sauce

chunky pasta sauce

Prep: 20 min. / **Cook:** 1 hour

Edythe Hawkinson, Tumwater, Washington

A cousin of mine was the first one in our family to make this meatless spaghetti sauce. With the thick sauce's veggies and great garlic and herb flavor, you don't miss the meat.

- 1 large onion, chopped
- 1 large green pepper, chopped
- 2 celery ribs, chopped
- 2 tablespoons olive oil
- 1 can (6 ounces) pitted ripe olives, drained and sliced
- 6 garlic cloves, minced
- 4 teaspoons beef bouillon granules
- 1 cup hot water
- 2 cans (15 ounces *each*) tomato sauce
- 1 can (28 ounces) diced tomatoes, undrained
- 1 can (6 ounces) tomato paste
- 1 jar (6 ounces) sliced mushrooms, drained
- 2 teaspoons dried basil
- 2 teaspoons dried oregano
- 1/2 teaspoon salt, optional
- 1/2 teaspoon pepper
- Hot cooked pasta

In a Dutch oven, saute the onion, green pepper and celery in oil until vegetables are tender. Add olives and garlic; cook 1 minute longer.

Dissolve bouillon in hot water; add to vegetable mixture. Stir in the tomato sauce, tomatoes, tomato paste, mushrooms, basil, oregano, salt if desired and pepper.

Bring to a boil. Reduce heat; cover. Simmer for 1 hour, stirring occasionally. Serve with pasta. **Yield: 12-14 servings.**

alfredo chicken tortellini

Prep/Total Time: 30 min.

Tiffany Treanor, Waukomis, Oklahoma

I'm always trying to come up with something new, and for this recipe, I just started putting things together. I was surprised how good it tasted.

1-1/2	cups frozen cheese tortellini
1	boneless skinless chicken breast half (6 ounces), cut into 1-inch cubes
3	bacon strips, chopped
1/8	teaspoon adobo seasoning
1/3	cup chopped onion
1/3	cup chopped sweet red pepper
3	teaspoons minced garlic
1	can (10-3/4 ounces) condensed cream of chicken soup, undiluted
1/2	cup 2% milk
1/3	cup sour cream
2	tablespoons grated Parmesan cheese
1	cup frozen chopped broccoli, thawed and drained

Cook tortellini according to package directions. Meanwhile, in a large saucepan, cook and stir the chicken, bacon and adobo seasoning over medium heat until chicken is no longer pink. Add onion and red pepper; cook and stir until tender. Add garlic; cook 1 minute longer.

In a small bowl, combine the soup, milk, sour cream and cheese; stir into chicken mixture. Bring to a boil. Reduce heat; simmer, uncovered, for 5-7 minutes.

Drain tortellini; add to chicken mixture. Stir in broccoli; heat through. **Yield: 3 servings.**

ravioli skillet

alfredo chicken tortellini

ravioli skillet

Prep/Total Time: 30 min.

Taste of Home Test Kitchen

Short on time? Our staff discovered that prosciutto and mozzarella cheese can dress up store-bought ravioli in mere minutes. If you prefer, store-bought refrigerated or frozen tortellini works just as well.

1	pound ground beef
3/4	cup chopped green pepper
1	ounce prosciutto *or* deli ham, chopped
3	cups spaghetti sauce
3/4	cup water
1	package (25 ounces) frozen cheese ravioli
1	cup (4 ounces) shredded part-skim mozzarella cheese

In a large skillet, cook the beef, green pepper and prosciutto over medium heat until meat is no longer pink; drain.

Stir in spaghetti sauce and water; bring to a boil. Add the ravioli. Reduce heat; cover and simmer for 7-9 minutes or until ravioli is tender, stirring once. Sprinkle with cheese. Simmer, uncovered, 1-2 minutes longer or until cheese is melted. **Yield: 4 servings.**

Tip! *meet prosciutto*

Not familiar with prosciutto? The thinly sliced meat is an Italian-style ham that's salt-cured and air-dried for 10 months to 2 years. It can be served in a variety of ways, but most often, you'll find it served on an antipasto platter, or wrapped around a slice of melon. It's also eaten as accompaniment to cooked spring veggies and mixed into pasta dishes.

fresh tomato pasta toss

Prep/Total Time: 30 min.

Cheryl Travagliante, Cleveland, Ohio

Dipping whole tomatoes into boiling water makes them easier to peel for this summertime pasta specialty. Sprinkle the finished results with shredded Parmesan cheese and enjoy.

- 3 **pounds ripe fresh tomatoes**
- 1 **package (16 ounces) uncooked penne pasta**
- 2 **garlic cloves, minced**
- 1 **tablespoon canola oil**
- 1 **tablespoon minced fresh parsley *or* 1 teaspoon dried parsley flakes**
- 1 **tablespoon minced fresh basil *or* 1 teaspoon dried basil**
- 2 **teaspoons minced fresh oregano *or* 3/4 teaspoon dried oregano**
- 1 **teaspoon salt**
- 1/4 **teaspoon sugar**
- 1/8 **teaspoon pepper**
- 1/4 **cup heavy whipping cream**
- 1/4 **cup shredded Parmesan *or* Romano cheese**

To remove peels from tomatoes, fill a large saucepan with water and bring to a boil. Place tomatoes, one at a time, in boiling water for 30 seconds. Immediately plunge in ice water. Peel skins with a sharp paring knife and discard. Chop pulp; set aside.

Cook penne pasta according to package directions. In a large skillet, cook garlic in oil over medium heat for 1 minute or until tender. Add the parsley, basil, oregano, salt, sugar, pepper and reserved tomato pulp. Bring to a boil; reduce heat. Add cream; heat through.

Drain pasta and transfer to a serving bowl. Pour the tomato sauce over pasta; toss to coat. Sprinkle with Parmesan cheese. **Yield: 8 servings.**

chicken orzo skillet

Prep/Total Time: 30 min.

Kathleen Farrell, Rochester, New York

As a busy homemaker with a home-based business, I try to make dinners that are quick and healthy for my gang. I combined two standby recipes to come up with this new family favorite.

- 1 **cup uncooked orzo pasta**
- 1 **pound boneless skinless chicken breasts, cubed**
- 3 **teaspoons olive oil, *divided***
- 3 **garlic cloves, minced**
- 2 **cans (14-1/2 ounces *each*) stewed tomatoes, cut up**
- 1 **can (15 ounces) white kidney *or* cannellini beans, rinsed and drained**
- 1-1/2 **teaspoons Italian seasoning**
- 1/2 **teaspoon salt**
- 1 **package (16 ounces) frozen broccoli florets, thawed**

Cook orzo according to package directions. Meanwhile, in a large nonstick skillet coated with cooking spray, cook chicken in 2 teaspoons oil for 6-7 minutes or until no longer pink. Remove and keep warm.

In the same skillet, cook garlic in remaining oil for 1 minute or until tender. Stir in the tomatoes, beans, Italian seasoning and salt. Bring to a boil. Stir in broccoli and chicken; heat through. Drain orzo; stir into chicken mixture. **Yield: 6 servings.**

no-cook herbed tomato sauce

no-cook herbed tomato sauce

Prep/Total Time: 20 min.

Taste of Home Test Kitchen

This lip-smacking sauce, compliments of our home economists, is a wonderful way to use tomatoes, basil and green onions from your garden. Because it requires no cooking, it won't cause you to heat up the stove on warm summer days.

- 5 medium tomatoes (about 1-1/2 pounds), chopped
- 1/4 cup snipped fresh basil
- 1/2 cup chopped green onions
- 2 garlic cloves, minced
- 1 tablespoon olive oil

Salt and pepper to taste

Hot cooked pasta

Grated Parmesan cheese

In a large bowl, combine the tomatoes, basil, onions, garlic, oil, salt and pepper. Let stand at room temperature for 30-60 minutes, stirring occasionally. Serve with pasta. Sprinkle with cheese. **Yield: 3 cups.**

linguine with fresh tomatoes

Prep/Total Time: 15 min.

Susan Jones, Downers Grove, Illinois

This medley is brimming with robust garlic and basil and is a wonderful way to use your bounty of late-summer tomatoes. It's ideal as a side dish for grilled chicken, but also as a great light supper when coupled with a salad and breadsticks.

- 8 ounces uncooked linguine
- 3 medium tomatoes, chopped
- 6 green onions, sliced
- 1/2 cup grated Parmesan cheese

- 1/4 cup minced fresh basil *or* 4 teaspoons dried basil
- 2 garlic cloves, minced
- 1 teaspoon salt
- 1/2 teaspoon pepper
- 3 tablespoons butter

Cook pasta according to package directions. Meanwhile, in a large serving bowl, combine the tomatoes, onions, Parmesan cheese, basil, garlic, salt and pepper. Drain pasta and toss with butter. Add to tomato mixture; toss to coat. **Yield: 6 servings.**

pasta primavera

Prep/Total Time: 25 min.

Clara DelVitto, Midlothian, Virginia

I eat very little meat, so I'm always on the lookout for vegetarian and low-fat recipes. I came up with this winner after some trial and error. Its summer-like flavor shines through in every bite.

- 1/2 cup sliced onion
- 1/2 cup julienned green *or* sweet red pepper
- 2 teaspoons olive oil
- 1/2 cup sliced zucchini
- 1/2 cup sliced yellow summer squash
- 2 medium fresh mushrooms, sliced
- 3/4 cup stewed tomatoes
- 1/4 to 1/2 teaspoon dried basil
- 2 cups hot cooked pasta

Shredded Parmesan cheese, optional

In a large skillet, saute onion and green pepper in oil until crisp-tender. Add the zucchini, yellow squash and mushrooms; saute for 1 minute. Add tomatoes and basil. Bring to a boil; reduce heat. Cover and simmer for 8-10 minutes or until vegetables are tender. Toss with pasta; sprinkle with cheese if desired. **Yield: 2 servings.**

pasta primavera

meat, poultry & seafood

pesto rice-stuffed pork chops / page 77

Savor robust flavor in every bite of these entrees. Whether your choice is beef, pork, chicken or seafood, these recipes will help you create restaurant-style fare in the comfort of your own home.

parmesan chicken 74

salmon with fettuccine alfredo 74

chicken piccata 75

chicken cacciatore 76

pork italiano 76

pesto rice-stuffed pork chops 77

chicken parmigiana 77

italian strip steaks with focaccia 78

herbed shrimp fettuccine 78

red pepper & parmesan tilapia 78

chicken marsala with pasta 79

shrimp and olive rigatoni 79

tilapia florentine 80

saucy beef roast 81

pesto halibut 81

smothered chicken 81

bruschetta chicken 82

mushroom pork scallopini 82

seafood fettuccine 82

chicken milan 83

italian pot roast 83

parmesan chicken

parmesan chicken

Prep/Total Time: 20 min.

Margie Eddy, Ann Arbor, Michigan

I like to make this poultry specialty when I have extra spaghetti sauce on hand. The herbed coating on the tender chicken turns nice and golden.

- 1/2 cup seasoned bread crumbs
- 1/2 cup grated Parmesan cheese, *divided*
- 1-1/2 teaspoons dried oregano, *divided*
- 1/2 teaspoon dried basil
- 1/2 teaspoon salt
- 1/4 teaspoon pepper
- 1 egg
- 1 tablespoon water
- 4 boneless skinless chicken breast halves (4 ounces *each*)
- 2 tablespoons butter
- 2 cups meatless spaghetti sauce
- 1/2 teaspoon garlic salt
- 1 cup (4 ounces) shredded part-skim mozzarella cheese

Hot cooked fettuccine *or* pasta of your choice

In a shallow bowl, combine the bread crumbs, 1/4 cup Parmesan cheese, 1 teaspoon oregano, basil, salt and pepper. In another shallow bowl, combine the egg and water. Dip chicken in egg mixture, then coat with crumb mixture.

In a large skillet, cook chicken in butter on both sides until a meat thermometer reads 170°.

Meanwhile, in a large saucepan, combine the spaghetti sauce, garlic salt and remaining oregano. Cook over medium heat until heated through. Spoon sauce over chicken; sprinkle with mozzarella cheese and remaining Parmesan cheese. Serve chicken with pasta. **Yield: 4 servings.**

salmon with fettuccine alfredo

Prep/Total Time: 30 min.

Pat Patty, Spring, Texas

A little imagination helped me come up with a smart twist on an Italian classic that used salmon instead of chicken. This healthy and elegant entree makes a pretty dish fit for company and special celebrations.

- 4 salmon fillets (4 ounces *each*)
- 1/4 teaspoon coarsely ground pepper, *divided*
- 4 ounces uncooked fettuccine
- 2 garlic cloves, minced
- 1 tablespoon reduced-fat margarine
- 1 tablespoon all-purpose flour
- 1/8 teaspoon salt
- 1 cup fat-free milk
- 4 tablespoons grated Parmesan cheese, *divided*

Place salmon, skin side down, on a broiler rack coated with cooking spray. Sprinkle salmon with 1/8 teaspoon pepper. Broil 4-6 in. from the heat for 10-12 minutes or until fish flakes easily with a fork. Meanwhile, cook fettuccine according to package directions.

In a small saucepan, cook garlic in margarine for 1 minute or until tender. Stir in flour, salt and remaining pepper; gradually stir in milk. Bring to a boil; cook and stir for 2 minutes or until thickened. Remove from the heat. Stir in 3 tablespoons Parmesan cheese.

Drain fettuccine; toss with sauce. Serve with salmon. Sprinkle with remaining cheese. **Yield: 4 servings.**

Editor's Note: This recipe was tested with Parkay Light stick margarine.

salmon with fettuccine alfredo

chicken piccata

Prep/Total Time: 25 min.

Cynthia Heil, Augusta, Georgia

Laced with lemon and simmered in white wine, this easy stovetop entree couldn't be more impressive. And yet, it's on the table in less than half an hour. Its ease and melt-in-your-mouth flavor make it a perfect addition to your weeknight meal lineup.

4	boneless skinless chicken breast halves (4 ounces *each*)
1/4	cup all-purpose flour
1/2	teaspoon salt
1/2	teaspoon pepper
1/4	cup butter, cubed
1/4	cup white wine *or* chicken broth
1	tablespoon lemon juice

Flatten chicken to 1/2-in. thickness. In a large resealable plastic bag, combine the flour, salt and pepper. Add chicken, one piece at a time, and shake to coat.

In a large skillet, brown chicken over medium heat in butter. Stir in wine. Bring to a boil. Reduce heat; simmer, uncovered, for 12-15 minutes or until chicken is no longer pink. Drizzle with lemon juice. **Yield: 4 servings.**

chicken cacciatore

Prep: 20 min. / **Cook:** 4 hours

Denise Hollebeke, Penhold, Alberta

Here's an Italian specialty made easy in the slow cooker! Dried herbs and fresh garlic give it an aromatic flavor. And green pepper, sliced mushrooms and diced tomatoes do a fine job of rounding out the juicy chicken entree.

- 1/3 cup all-purpose flour
- 1 broiler/fryer chicken (3 to 4 pounds), cut up
- 2 tablespoons canola oil
- 2 medium onions, cut into wedges
- 1 medium green pepper, cut into strips
- 1 jar (6 ounces) sliced mushrooms, drained
- 1 can (14-1/2 ounces) diced tomatoes, undrained
- 2 garlic cloves, minced
- 1/2 teaspoon salt
- 1/2 teaspoon dried oregano
- 1/4 teaspoon dried basil
- 1/2 cup shredded Parmesan cheese

Place flour in a large resealable plastic bag. Add chicken, a few pieces at a time, and shake to coat. In a large skillet, brown chicken in oil on all sides.

Transfer to a 5-qt. slow cooker. Top with onions, green pepper and mushrooms. In a small bowl, combine the tomatoes, garlic, salt, oregano and basil; pour over vegetables. Cover and cook on low for 4-5 hours or until chicken juices run clear and vegetables are tender. Serve with cheese. **Yield: 6 servings.**

pork italiano

chicken cacciatore

pork italiano

Prep/Total Time: 30 min.

Julee Wallberg, Salt Lake City, Utah

It's simple to bring home the essence of Italy with this tantalizing parmigiana pork entree. Baked in mere minutes, the crispy yet moist pork tenderloin makes a simply satisfying dinner your family will request often.

- 1-1/3 cups uncooked spiral pasta
- 2 cups meatless spaghetti sauce
- 1 pork tenderloin (1 pound)
- 1/4 cup egg substitute
- 1/3 cup seasoned bread crumbs
- 3 tablespoons grated Parmesan cheese, *divided*
- 1/4 cup shredded part-skim mozzarella cheese

Cook pasta according to package directions. Place spaghetti sauce in a small saucepan; cook over low heat until heated through, stirring occasionally.

Meanwhile, cut tenderloin into eight slices; flatten to 1/4-in. thickness. Place egg substitute in a shallow bowl. In another shallow bowl, combine bread crumbs and 1 tablespoon Parmesan cheese. Dip pork slices in egg substitute, then roll in crumb mixture.

Place pork on a baking sheet coated with cooking spray. Bake at 425° for 5-6 minutes on each side or until the meat is no longer pink.

Drain pasta; serve with spaghetti sauce and pork. Sprinkle with mozzarella cheese and remaining Parmesan cheese. **Yield: 4 servings.**

pesto rice-stuffed pork chops

Prep: 20 min. / **Bake:** 25 min.

Carolyn Popwell, Lacey, Washington

My family loves pork chops so I experimented with this stuffed version. I used a homemade pesto, rice and cheese mixture to produce a meal with winning results.

1/2	cup fresh basil leaves
1/2	cup fresh parsley sprigs
1/2	cup chopped pecans
3	garlic cloves, peeled
2/3	cup cooked wild rice
2	tablespoons grated Parmesan cheese
2	tablespoons cream cheese, softened
1	tablespoon olive oil
1	teaspoon chili sauce
4	bone-in pork loin chops (8 ounces *each*)
1/2	teaspoon lemon-pepper seasoning
1	tablespoon butter

In a food processor, combine the basil, parsley, pecans and garlic; cover and process until blended. Transfer to a small bowl; add the rice, cheeses, oil and chili sauce.

Cut a pocket in each pork chop by slicing almost to the bone. Sprinkle chops with lemon-pepper.

In a large skillet, brown chops in butter; cool for 5 minutes. Fill with rice mixture; secure with toothpicks if necessary. Place in a 13-in. x 9-in. baking dish coated with cooking spray.

Bake pork chops, uncovered, at 350° for 28-32 minutes or until a meat thermometer reads 160°. Discard the toothpicks. **Yield: 4 servings.**

pesto rice-stuffed pork chops

chicken parmigiana

chicken parmigiana

Prep: 15 min. / **Cook:** 20 min.

Iola Butler, Sun City, California

For years my husband ordered Chicken Parmigiana whenever we ate at restaurants. Then I found this recipe, adjusted it for two and began making it at home. It's still his first choice.

1	can (15 ounces) tomato sauce
2	teaspoons Italian seasoning
1/2	teaspoon garlic powder
1	egg
1/4	cup seasoned bread crumbs
3	tablespoons grated Parmesan cheese
2	boneless skinless chicken breast halves (4 ounces *each*)
2	tablespoons olive oil
2	slices part-skim mozzarella cheese

In a small saucepan, combine the tomato sauce, Italian seasoning and garlic powder. Bring to a boil. Reduce heat; cover and simmer for 20 minutes.

Meanwhile, in a shallow bowl, lightly beat the egg. In another shallow bowl, combine bread crumbs and Parmesan cheese. Dip chicken in egg, then coat with crumb mixture.

In a large skillet, cook chicken in oil over medium heat for 5 minutes on each side or until a meat thermometer reads 170°. Top with mozzarella cheese. Cover and cook 3-4 minutes longer or until cheese is melted. Serve with tomato sauce. **Yield: 2 servings.**

Tip! *seasoning basics*

You'll find Italian seasoning in the spice aisle of most stores. To make your own, substitute 1/4 teaspoon each of basil, thyme, rosemary and oregano for each teaspoon of Italian seasoning.

italian strip steaks with focaccia

Prep: 15 min. / **Cook:** 25 min.

Patricia Harmon, Baden, Pennsylvania

This simple dinner recipe lets the host enjoy entertaining. It comes together quickly and makes a beautiful presentation. Fans of Italian food will be impressed with the flavor.

- 4 boneless beef top loin steaks (8 ounces *each*)
- 3 tablespoons olive oil, *divided*
- 1/2 pound sliced baby portobello mushrooms
- 1 shallot, finely chopped
- 3 tablespoons chopped red onion
- 2 garlic cloves, minced
- 2 teaspoons minced fresh rosemary
- 1/2 cup roasted sweet red peppers, cut into strips
- 1/4 cup dry red wine *or* beef broth
- 1/4 teaspoon salt
- 1/4 teaspoon coarsely ground pepper
- 1 focaccia bread (12 ounces), cut into quarters
- 2/3 cup shredded Asiago cheese
- 1/4 cup sliced pimiento-stuffed olives

In a large skillet, cook steaks in 2 tablespoons oil over medium heat for 5-6 minutes on each side or until meat reaches desired doneness (for medium-rare, a meat thermometer should read 145°; medium, 160°; well-done, 170°). Remove and keep warm.

In the same skillet, saute the mushrooms, shallot and onion in remaining oil. Add garlic and rosemary; saute 1-2 minutes longer. Stir in the roasted sweet red peppers, wine, salt and pepper; heat through.

Place focaccia on serving plates; top each with a steak and 1/2 cup mushroom mixture. Sprinkle with cheese and olives. **Yield: 4 servings.**

Editor's Note: Top loin steak may be labeled as strip steak, Kansas City steak, New York strip steak, ambassador steak or boneless club steak in your region.

herbed shrimp fettuccine

Prep/Total Time: 30 min.

Marilyn Weaver, Sparks, Maryland

Everyone will think you went out of your way when you serve this elegant seafood entree. You'll be amazed at the dish's effortless preparation. We've been enjoying it for years.

- 6 ounces fettuccine *or* medium egg noodles
- 1 envelope herb and garlic soup mix
- 1-3/4 cups milk
- 1 pound uncooked shrimp, peeled and deveined
- 2 cups broccoli florets
- 1/4 cup grated Parmesan cheese

Cook fettuccine according to package directions. Meanwhile, combine soup mix and milk in a saucepan. Cook and stir over medium heat until smooth. Add shrimp and broccoli; simmer, uncovered, for 3-5 minutes or until shrimp are pink (do not boil). Drain pasta; toss with shrimp mixture. Sprinkle with cheese. **Yield: 4 servings.**

red pepper & parmesan tilapia

Prep/Total Time: 20 min.

Michelle Martin, Durham, North Carolina

My husband and I are always looking for light fish recipes because of their health benefits. This one's a hit thanks to the Italian-inspired seasonings.

- 1/4 cup egg substitute
- 1/2 cup grated Parmesan cheese
- 1 teaspoon Italian seasoning
- 1/2 to 1 teaspoon crushed red pepper flakes
- 1/2 teaspoon pepper
- 4 tilapia fillets (6 ounces *each*)

Place the egg substitute in a shallow bowl. In another shallow bowl, combine the Parmesan cheese, Italian seasoning, pepper flakes and pepper. Dip the fillets in egg substitute, then the cheese mixture.

Place in a 15-in. x 10-in. x 1-in. baking pan coated with cooking spray. Bake at 425° for 10-15 minutes or until fish flakes easily with a fork. **Yield: 4 servings.**

chicken marsala with pasta

Prep/Total Time: 30 min.

Trisha Kruse, Eagle, Idaho

This dish is fancy enough for special occasions, but speedy and easy for weeknight meals. My family always looks forward to this chicken. Using leftover broiled chicken breasts works fine and saves you time, too.

2	cups sliced fresh mushrooms
1/4	cup butter, *divided*
2	teaspoons minced garlic
2-1/4	cups hot water
1/4	cup marsala wine *or* chicken broth
1	envelope (4.3 ounces) fettuccini and chicken-flavored sauce mix
4	boneless skinless chicken breast halves (4 ounces *each*)
1/4	cup all-purpose flour
1/4	teaspoon salt
1/4	teaspoon pepper
1	tablespoon canola oil
2	tablespoons sour cream

In a large saucepan, saute mushrooms in 2 tablespoons butter for 4-5 minutes or until tender. Add garlic; cook 1 minute longer. Add water and wine. Bring to a boil; stir in pasta mix. Reduce heat; simmer, uncovered, for 10 minutes or until pasta is tender.

Meanwhile, flatten chicken to 1/2-in. thickness. In a large resealable plastic bag, combine the flour, salt and pepper. Add chicken, a few pieces at a time, and shake to coat.

In a large skillet, cook chicken in oil and remaining butter over medium heat for 4-5 minutes on each side or until no longer pink. Remove pasta mixture from the heat. Stir in sour cream. Serve with chicken. **Yield: 4 servings.**

chicken marsala with pasta

shrimp and olive rigatoni

Prep: 20 min. / **Cook:** 20 min.

Elaine Sweet, Dallas, Texas

This pasta entree is one of my gang's preferred dinners. Even those who don't usually care for shrimp can't resist it when it's prepared in this regal main dish.

12	ounces uncooked rigatoni *or* large tube pasta
3	garlic cloves, minced
2	green onions, chopped
1	tablespoon olive oil
1	pound uncooked medium shrimp, peeled and deveined
3	tablespoons white wine *or* reduced-sodium chicken broth
1/4	cup minced fresh basil
2	tablespoons minced fresh parsley
1	teaspoon grated lemon peel
1/2	teaspoon salt
1/4	teaspoon coarsely ground pepper
1/4	teaspoon crushed red pepper flakes
1	can (2-1/4 ounces) sliced ripe olives, drained
1/2	cup sliced pimiento-stuffed olives
2	anchovy fillets, rinsed, drained and chopped
5	plum tomatoes, seeded and chopped
1	jar (2 ounces) sliced pimientos, drained
1/3	cup shredded Parmesan cheese

Additional fresh basil, optional

Cook pasta according to package directions. Meanwhile, in a large nonstick skillet coated with cooking spray, saute garlic and onions in oil for 1 minute. Add shrimp and wine or broth; cook for 3-5 minutes or until shrimp turn pink.

Remove from the heat; stir in the basil, parsley, lemon peel, salt, pepper and crushed red pepper flakes. Add the olives and anchovies.

Drain the pasta; stir into skillet. Add tomatoes and pimientos; return to the heat and heat through. Sprinkle with Parmesan cheese. Garnish pasta with basil leaves if desired. **Yield: 6 servings.**

tilapia florentine

Prep/Total Time: 30 min.

Melanie Bachman, Ulysses, Pennsylvania

Looking for a way to get a little more heart-healthy fish into your family's weekly diet? You'll win them over with this pleasing entree. Topped with fresh spinach and a splash of lime, it's sure to become a frequent dinner request!

1	package (6 ounces) fresh baby spinach
6	teaspoons canola oil, *divided*
4	tilapia fillets (4 ounces *each*)
2	tablespoons lime juice
2	teaspoons garlic-herb seasoning blend
1	egg, lightly beaten
1/2	cup part-skim ricotta cheese
1/4	cup grated Parmesan cheese

In a large nonstick skillet, cook spinach in 4 teaspoons oil until wilted; drain. Meanwhile, place tilapia in a greased 13-in. x 9-in. baking dish. Drizzle with lime juice and remaining oil. Sprinkle with seasoning blend.

In a small bowl, combine the egg, ricotta cheese and spinach; spoon over fillets. Sprinkle with Parmesan cheese.

Bake at 375° for 15-20 minutes or until fish flakes easily with a fork. **Yield: 4 servings.**

saucy italian roast

saucy beef roast

Prep: 10 min. / Cook: 8 hours

Jan Roat, Red Lodge, Montana

This tender roast is a choice set-and-forget meal. I thicken the juices with a little flour and add ketchup, then serve the sauce and beef slices over pasta.

- 1 beef rump roast *or* bottom round roast (3 to 3-1/2 pounds)
- 1/2 to 1 teaspoon salt
- 1/2 teaspoon garlic powder
- 1/4 teaspoon pepper
- 1 jar (4-1/2 ounces) sliced mushrooms, drained
- 1 medium onion, diced
- 1 jar (14 ounces) spaghetti sauce
- 1/4 to 1/2 cup red wine *or* beef broth

Hot cooked pasta

Cut the roast in half. Combine the salt, garlic powder and pepper; rub over roast. Place in a 5-qt. slow cooker. Top with mushrooms and onion. Combine the spaghetti sauce and wine; pour over meat and vegetables.

Cover and cook on low for 8-9 hours or until the meat is tender. Slice roast; serve roast with hot cooked pasta and pan juices. **Yield: 10 servings.**

pesto halibut

Prep/Total Time: 20 min.

April Showalter, Milwaukee, Wisconsin

The mildness of the halibut fillet complements the deep flavor of pesto perfectly. It literally takes 5 minutes to get the fish fillets ready for the oven, so you can start on your choice of side dishes while the main dish bakes.

- 2 tablespoons olive oil
- 1 envelope pesto sauce mix
- 1 tablespoon lemon juice
- 6 halibut fillets (4 ounces *each*)

In a small bowl, combine the oil, sauce mix and lemon juice; brush over both sides of fillets. Place in a greased 13-in. x 9-in. baking dish.

Bake, uncovered, at 450° for 12-15 minutes or until fish flakes easily with a fork. **Yield: 6 servings.**

smothered chicken

Prep: 15 min. / Bake: 20 min.

Mary Kretschmer, Miami, Florida

This is one of my husband's favorites and has become a staple in our house. The chicken entree is tasty but requires little fuss.

- 1/2 teaspoon dried oregano
- 1/4 teaspoon garlic powder
- 1/4 teaspoon salt, *divided*
- 1/4 teaspoon pepper, *divided*
- 4 boneless skinless chicken breast halves (4 ounces *each*)
- 2 teaspoons canola oil
- 1 cup part-skim ricotta cheese
- 1 cup crushed tomatoes
- 4 slices part-skim mozzarella cheese

In a small bowl, combine the oregano, garlic powder, 1/8 teaspoon salt and 1/8 teaspoon pepper; rub over chicken. In a large nonstick skillet coated with cooking spray, brown chicken in oil for 3-4 minutes on each side.

Transfer to an 11-in. x 7-in. baking dish coated with cooking spray. Combine ricotta cheese and remaining salt and pepper; spoon over chicken. Top with tomatoes.

Bake, uncovered, at 350° for 15 minutes. Top with cheese. Bake 5-10 minutes longer or a meat thermometer reads 170°. **Yield: 4 servings.**

smothered chicken

bruschetta chicken

bruschetta chicken

Prep: 10 min. / **Bake:** 30 min.

Carolin Cattoi-Demkiw, Lethbridge, Alberta

My husband and I enjoy serving this tomato-covered chicken to company as well as family. It looks like we fussed, but it's fast, simple and satisfying.

- 1/2 cup all-purpose flour
- 2 eggs, lightly beaten
- 1/4 cup dry bread crumbs
- 1/4 cup grated Parmesan cheese
- 4 boneless skinless chicken breast halves (6 ounces *each*)
- 1 tablespoon butter, melted
- 2 large tomatoes, seeded and chopped
- 3 tablespoons minced fresh basil
- 1 tablespoon olive oil
- 2 garlic cloves, minced
- 1/2 teaspoon salt
- 1/4 teaspoon pepper

Place flour and eggs in separate shallow bowls. In a third bowl, combine bread crumbs and cheese. Dip chicken in flour, then eggs; coat with bread crumb mixture.

Place in a greased 13-in. x 9-in. baking dish. Drizzle with butter. Bake, uncovered, at 375° for 25-30 minutes or until a meat thermometer reads 170°.

In a small bowl, combine the remaining ingredients. Spoon over the chicken. Return to the oven for 3-5 minutes or until tomato mixture is heated through. **Yield: 4 servings.**

mushroom pork scallopini

Prep: 10 min. / **Bake:** 30 min.

Carol Ebner, Fort Dodge, Iowa

Tender pork has fantastic flavor when coated with a buttery sauce seasoned with garlic and herbs. This recipe serves a crowd, so I make it often for guests.

- 3 to 4 pork tenderloins (about 1 pound *each*), cut into 1-inch slices
- 1 cup all-purpose flour
- 1/4 cup butter, cubed
- 1/4 cup canola oil
- 1 cup white wine *or* chicken broth
- 1/2 cup water
- 1 large onion, chopped
- 1 to 2 garlic cloves, minced
- 1/2 teaspoon salt
- 1/2 teaspoon pepper
- 1/2 teaspoon *each* dried thyme, oregano and rosemary, crushed
- 1 pound fresh mushrooms, sliced

Hot cooked fettuccine

Dredge pork slices in flour. In a large skillet, heat butter and oil. Brown pork on both sides in batches; remove and keep warm. Stir in the wine, water, onion, garlic and seasonings into drippings. Return pork to skillet, layering if necessary. Top with mushrooms.

Cover and cook on low heat for 15-20 minutes or until meat is no longer pink. Serve with fettuccine. **Yield: 8-10 servings.**

seafood fettuccine

Prep/Total Time: 15 min.

Kim Jorgensen, Coulee City, Washington

Shrimp gives an elegant touch to this rich and creamy pasta dish. It's a comforting entree. It's also delicious using scallops or crabmeat in place of the shrimp.

- 3/4 pound uncooked medium shrimp, peeled and deveined
- 1 can (4 ounces) mushroom stems and pieces, drained
- 1/2 teaspoon garlic powder
- 1/8 teaspoon salt
- 1/8 teaspoon pepper
- 1/4 cup butter, cubed
- 1 package (8 ounces) fettuccine, cooked and drained
- 1/2 cup grated Parmesan cheese
- 1/2 cup milk
- 1/2 cup sour cream

Minced fresh parsley, optional

In a large saucepan, saute the shrimp, mushrooms, garlic powder, salt and pepper in butter for 3-5 minutes. Stir in the fettuccine, cheese, milk and sour cream. Cook over medium heat for 3-5 minutes or until heated through (do not boil). Sprinkle with parsley if desired. **Yield: 4 servings.**

Editor's Note: Scallops or crab may be substituted for half of the shrimp.

chicken milan

Prep/Total Time: 20 min.

Lara Priest, Gansevoort, New York

Lightly breaded and sauteed chicken breast strips are tossed with tender linguine pasta for a main meal that tastes like restaurant fare. Best of all, it's ready to eat in under 30 minutes.

- 8 ounces uncooked linguine
- 1 tablespoon minced garlic
- 3 tablespoons olive oil, *divided*
- 1/2 teaspoon dried parsley flakes
- 1/2 teaspoon pepper, *divided*
- 1/4 cup all-purpose flour
- 1 teaspoon dried basil
- 1/2 teaspoon salt
- 2 eggs
- 1-1/2 pounds boneless skinless chicken breasts, cut into strips

Cook linguine according to package directions. Meanwhile, in a large skillet, saute garlic in 1 tablespoon oil for 1 minute or until tender; stir in parsley and 1/4 teaspoon pepper. Remove to a small bowl and set aside.

In a shallow bowl, combine the flour, basil, salt and the remaining pepper. In another shallow bowl, whisk the eggs. Dredge chicken strips in flour mixture, then dip in eggs.

In the same skillet, cook chicken in remaining oil over medium-high heat for 8-10 minutes or until no longer pink. Drain linguine and place on a serving platter. Pour reserved garlic mixture over linguine and toss to coat; top with chicken. **Yield: 6 servings.**

chicken milan

italian pot roast

italian pot roast

Prep: 20 min. / **Bake:** 2 hours

Carolyn Wells, North Syracuse, New York

I had so many requests for this recipe that I made up cards to hand out when I served it at get-togethers. It's my husband and son's favorite main dish.

- 1 tablespoon all-purpose flour
- 1 large oven roasting bag
- 1 boneless beef chuck roast (3 pounds)
- 1-2/3 cups water
- 1 can (10-3/4 ounces) condensed tomato soup, undiluted
- 1 envelope onion soup mix
- 1-1/2 teaspoons Italian seasoning
- 1 garlic clove, minced
- 1/4 cup cornstarch
- 1/4 cup cold water

Sprinkle flour into oven bag; shake to coat. Place in a 13-in. x 9-in. baking pan; add roast. In a small bowl, combine the water, tomato soup, soup mix, Italian seasoning and garlic; pour into oven bag.

Cut six 1/2-in. slits in top of bag; close with tie provided. Bake at 325° for 2 to 2-1/2 hours or until meat is tender.

Remove roast to a serving platter and keep warm. Transfer cooking juices to a small saucepan; skim fat. Bring to a boil. Combine cornstarch and cold water until smooth; stir into cooking juices. Return to a boil; cook and stir for 2 minutes or until thickened. Slice roast; serve with gravy. **Yield: 8-10 servings (3 cups gravy).**

pizzas

baked potato pizza / page 90

When the moon hits your eye like a big pizza pie...
It will be "amore" at first bite when you taste these homemade pizzas. From the classics to adventurous new tastes, your kitchen will be your favorite pizzeria.

caramelized onion-gorgonzola pizza 86

homemade pizza 86

tomato cheese pizza 87

chicken pesto pizza 87

pepperoni provolone pizzas 88

pesto sausage pizza makeover 89

effortless alfredo pizza 89

baked potato pizza 90

bacon-olive tomato pizza 90

shrimp pizza 90

alfredo bacon mushroom pizza 91

tomato spinach pizza 91

chicken fajita pizza 92

pizza lover's pie 92

pesto pizza 93

smoked salmon pizza 93

barbecued chicken pizza 93

rustic vegetarian pizza 93

spinach stuffed pizza 94

turkey pizza 94

two-meat pizza 95

bacon, lettuce & tomato pizza pie 95

caramelized onion-gorgonzola pizza

caramelized onion-gorgonzola pizza

Prep: 30 min. + rising / **Bake:** 20 min.

Taste of Home Test Kitchen

An all-time favorite recipe of our home economists, this gourmet-style pizza is surprisingly easy to prepare.

- 1 loaf (1 pound) frozen bread dough, thawed
- 2 tablespoons butter
- 2 tablespoons brown sugar
- 2 large sweet onions, thinly sliced and separated into rings
- 3 tablespoons olive oil
- 2 teaspoons dried basil
- 2 teaspoons dried oregano
- 1 teaspoon garlic powder
- 2 plum tomatoes, chopped
- 1 cup (4 ounces) shredded part-skim mozzarella cheese
- 3 ounces crumbled Gorgonzola *or* blue cheese
- 2 tablespoons grated Parmesan cheese
- 1/4 cup pitted Greek olives, chopped

Divide bread dough in half. Press each portion onto a 12-in. pizza pan coated with cooking spray; build up edges slightly. Prick dough several times with a fork. Cover and let rise in a warm place for 30 minutes.

Meanwhile, in a large skillet over medium heat, melt butter with brown sugar. Add onions; cook for 20-30 minutes or until golden brown, stirring occasionally.

Brush dough with oil. Combine the basil, oregano and garlic powder; sprinkle over dough. Bake at 425° for 10 minutes.

Arrange onions and tomatoes over crusts; sprinkle with cheeses and olives. Bake 8-10 minutes longer or until golden brown. **Yield: 2 pizzas (6 slices each).**

homemade pizza

Prep: 25 min. + rising / **Bake:** 25 min.

Marianne Edwards, Lake Stevens, Washington

Nothing beats the aroma of a homemade pizza baking in the oven. A seasoned tomato sauce is topped with a hearty beef mixture, green pepper and mozzarella cheese to create this mouthwatering main dish.

- 1 package (1/4 ounce) active dry yeast
- 1 teaspoon sugar
- 1-1/4 cups warm water (110° to 115°)
- 1/4 cup canola oil
- 1 teaspoon salt
- 3-1/2 cups all-purpose flour
- 1/2 pound ground beef
- 1 small onion, chopped
- 1 can (15 ounces) tomato sauce
- 3 teaspoons dried oregano
- 1 teaspoon dried basil
- 1 medium green pepper, diced
- 2 cups (8 ounces) shredded part-skim mozzarella cheese

In large bowl, dissolve yeast and sugar in water; let stand for 5 minutes. Add oil and salt. Stir in flour, a cup at a time, until a soft dough forms.

Turn onto floured surface; knead until smooth and elastic, about 2-3 minutes. Place in a greased bowl, turning once to grease top. Cover and let rise in a warm place until doubled, about 45 minutes. Meanwhile, cook beef and onion over medium heat until no longer pink; drain.

Punch down dough; divide in half. Press each into a greased 12-in. pizza pan. Combine the tomato sauce, oregano and basil; spread over each crust. Top with beef mixture, green pepper and cheese. Bake at 400° for 25-30 minutes or until crust is lightly browned. **Yield: 2 pizzas (6 servings).**

homemade pizza

tomato cheese pizza

tomato cheese pizza

Prep/Total Time: 30 min.

Greta Sawyers, Mount Airy, North Carolina

I've been making this cheesy delight for several years, and it's remained a favorite with family and friends. It can be used either as an effortless main dish or simple appetizer.

- 1 tube (13.8 ounces) refrigerated pizza crust
- 1 teaspoon minced garlic
- 2 cups (8 ounces) shredded part-skim mozzarella cheese
- 2/3 cup grated Romano cheese
- 2 teaspoons dried oregano
- 2 plum tomatoes, thinly sliced

Unroll pizza dough onto a greased 12-in. pizza pan; flatten dough and build up edges slightly. Spread garlic over crust. Bake at 375° for 7 minutes.

Sprinkle half of the cheeses and oregano over crust. Arrange the tomatoes on top. Sprinkle with remaining cheeses and oregano. Bake for 15-17 minutes or until crust is golden brown and cheese is melted. **Yield: 8 slices.**

chicken pesto pizza

Prep: 35 min. + rising / **Bake:** 20 min.

Heather Thompson, Woodland Hills, California

This is the only pizza I make—it even beats those from pizzeria establishments. Keeping the spices simple helps the flavor of the chicken and vegetables shine. Nothing's better than a pizza that tastes great and is good for you, too.

- 2 teaspoons active dry yeast
- 1 cup warm water (110° to 115°)
- 2-3/4 cups bread flour, *divided*
- 1 tablespoon plus 2 teaspoons olive oil, *divided*
- 1 tablespoon sugar
- 1-1/2 teaspoons salt, *divided*
- 1/2 pound boneless skinless chicken breasts, cut into 1/2-inch pieces
- 1 small onion, halved and thinly sliced
- 1/2 *each* small green, sweet red and yellow pepper, julienned
- 1/2 cup sliced fresh mushrooms
- 3 tablespoons prepared pesto
- 1-1/2 cups (6 ounces) shredded part-skim mozzarella cheese
- 1/4 teaspoon pepper

In a large bowl, dissolve yeast in warm water. Beat in 1 cup flour, 1 tablespoon oil, sugar and 1 teaspoon salt. Add the remaining flour; beat until combined.

Turn onto a lightly floured surface; knead until smooth and elastic, about 6-8 minutes. Place dough in a bowl coated with cooking spray, turning once to coat top. Cover and let rise in a warm place until doubled, about 1 hour.

In a large nonstick skillet over medium heat, cook the chicken, onion, peppers and mushrooms in remaining oil until chicken is no longer pink and vegetables are tender. Remove from the heat; set aside.

Punch dough down; roll into a 15-in. circle. Transfer to a 14-in. pizza pan. Build up edges slightly. Spread with pesto. Top with chicken mixture and cheese. Sprinkle with pepper and remaining salt.

Bake at 400° for 18-20 minutes or until crust and cheese are lightly browned. **Yield: 8 slices.**

chicken pesto pizza

pepperoni provolone pizzas

Prep/Total Time: 25 min.

Randy Armbruster, Waverly, Ohio

These tasty grilled pizzas use two kinds of sauce to create an enticing alternative to the usual brats and burgers served at summer parties.

- 1   can (13.8 ounces) refrigerated pizza crust
- 2   teaspoons olive oil
- 2/3 cup pizza sauce
- 1/2 cup prepared pesto
- 3   ounces sliced turkey pepperoni
- 1   large tomato, thinly sliced
- 3   cups (12 ounces) shredded provolone cheese

Using long-handled tongs, dip a paper towel in cooking oil and lightly coat the grill rack. Divide dough in half. On a lightly floured surface, roll each portion into a 12-in. x 10-in. rectangle.

Lightly brush both sides of dough with oil; place on grill. Cover and grill over medium heat for 1-2 minutes or until the bottom is lightly browned.

Remove from grill. Top the grilled side of each pizza with pizza sauce, pesto, pepperoni, tomato and cheese. Return to grill. Cover and cook each pizza for 4-5 minutes or until the bottom is lightly browned and cheese is melted. **Yield: 2 pizzas (4 pieces each).**

pesto sausage pizza makeover

Prep: 20 min. / **Bake:** 25 min.

Taste of Home Test Kitchen

Our home economists developed this quicker, healthier version of traditional sausage pizza. Frozen bread dough forms a tender crust that's spread with a yummy, creamy pesto sauce, and topped with Italian sausage, mushrooms, olives and cheese.

- 1/2 **pound bulk Italian sausage**
- 1 **cup chopped onion**
- 1 **loaf (1 pound) frozen bread dough, thawed**
- 1 **package (8 ounces) cream cheese, softened**
- 1/4 **cup prepared pesto**
- 1 **cup roasted garlic Parmesan spaghetti sauce**
- 2 **cups sliced fresh mushrooms**
- 1 **can (2-1/4 ounces) sliced ripe olives, drained**
- 1-1/2 **cups (6 ounces) shredded Monterey Jack cheese**

In a large skillet, cook sausage and onion over medium heat until meat is no longer pink; drain.

On a lightly floured surface, roll dough into a 16-in. x 11-in. rectangle. Transfer to a greased 15-in. x 10-in. x 1-in. baking pan. Build up edges slightly.

In a small bowl, beat cream cheese and pesto until blended. Spread over dough. Layer with spaghetti sauce, sausage mixture, mushrooms, olives and Monterey Jack cheese.

Bake at 400° for 25-30 minutes or until crust is golden brown and cheese is melted. **Yield: 12 slices.**

pesto sausage pizza makeover

effortless alfredo pizza

effortless alfredo pizza

Prep/Total Time: 20 min.

Brittney House, Lockport, Illinois

Here's a lighter, scrumptious pie for pizza night. The recipe makes great use of convenience products. While turkey, nutty fontina cheese and zippy red pepper flakes boost the flavor.

- 1 **package (10 ounces) frozen chopped spinach, thawed and squeezed dry**
- 1 **cup shredded cooked turkey breast**
- 2 **teaspoons lemon juice**
- 1/4 **teaspoon salt**
- 1/4 **teaspoon pepper**
- 1 **prebaked 12-inch pizza crust**
- 1 **garlic clove, peeled and halved**
- 1/2 **cup reduced-fat Alfredo sauce**
- 3/4 **cup shredded fontina cheese**
- 1/2 **teaspoon crushed red pepper flakes**

In a large bowl, combine the spinach, turkey, lemon juice, salt and pepper; set aside.

Place crust on an ungreased 12-in. pizza pan; rub with cut sides of garlic. Discard garlic. Spread Alfredo sauce over crust. Top with spinach mixture, cheese and pepper flakes.

Bake at 450° for 8-12 minutes or until crust is lightly browned. **Yield: 6 slices.**

Tip! *garlic alternatives*

There's really no substitute for garlic, which has a very distinctive flavor. If you don't like or have an allergy to garlic, you may choose to leave it out altogether or enhance the recipe with other herbs. In most cases, onion or chives add nice flavor to dishes that call for garlic.

baked potato pizza

Prep: 25 min. / **Bake:** 25 min.

Charlotte Hedke, Brownstown, Michigan

I wanted to re-create a lighter version of a restaurant menu item my friends, and I used to get all the time in college. Here's the hearty, cheesy, homemade version I developed.

- 3 medium potatoes, peeled and cut into 1/8-inch slices
- 1 loaf (1 pound) frozen pizza dough, thawed
- 3 tablespoons reduced-fat butter
- 4 garlic cloves, minced
- 1/4 teaspoon salt
- 1/4 teaspoon pepper
- 1 cup (4 ounces) shredded part-skim mozzarella cheese
- 1/4 cup shredded Parmigiano-Reggiano cheese
- 6 turkey bacon strips, cooked and crumbled
- 2 green onions, chopped
- 2 tablespoons minced chives

Reduced-fat sour cream, optional

Place potatoes in a small saucepan and cover with water. Bring to a boil. Reduce heat; cover and simmer for 15 minutes or until tender. Drain and pat dry.

Unroll dough onto a 14-in. pizza pan coated with cooking spray; flatten and build up edges slightly. In a microwave-safe bowl, melt butter with garlic; brush over dough.

Arrange potato slices in a single layer over dough; sprinkle with salt and pepper. Top with cheeses. Bake at 400° for 22-28 minutes or until crust is golden and cheese is melted.

Sprinkle with bacon, onions and chives. Serve with sour cream if desired. **Yield: 12 pieces.**

Editor's Note: This recipe was tested with Land O'Lakes light stick butter.

baked potato pizza

bacon-olive tomato pizza

Prep/Total Time: 30 min.

Cindy Clement, Colorado Springs, Colorado

By using bacon and tomatoes, I bring the flavor of a BLT to each delicious slice of this pizza. Black olives add a unique, but well-received twist. One bite will make this pie more popular than the usual pepperoni variety.

- 1 prebaked 12-inch pizza crust
- 1/3 cup ranch salad dressing
- 1 pound sliced bacon, cooked and crumbled
- 4 plum tomatoes, sliced
- 1 cup sliced fresh mushrooms
- 1 can (2-1/4 ounces) sliced ripe olives, drained
- 2 cups (8 ounces) shredded part-skim mozzarella cheese

Place crust on an ungreased 12-in. pizza pan. Top crust with dressing, bacon, tomatoes, mushrooms, olives and cheese. Bake at 450° for 10-12 minutes or until cheese is melted. **Yield: 8 slices.**

shrimp pizza

Prep/Total Time: 30 min.

Taste of Home Test Kitchen

Our home economists came up with this lighter pizza fit for seafood lovers! Fresh shrimp and melted cheese top the tender crust for a timely supper with a special touch.

- 1 tablespoon butter
- 4-1/2 teaspoons all-purpose flour
- 1/4 to 1/2 teaspoon ground mustard
- 1/8 to 1/4 teaspoon cayenne pepper
- 1/8 teaspoon salt
- 1 cup 2% milk
- 1 small onion, chopped
- 1 pound uncooked medium shrimp, peeled and deveined
- 1 prebaked 12-inch pizza crust
- 3/4 cup shredded part-skim mozzarella cheese

For white sauce, in a small nonstick saucepan, melt butter. Stir in the flour, mustard, cayenne and salt until smooth; gradually add milk. Bring to a boil; cook and stir for 2 minutes or until thickened. Remove from the heat; set aside.

In a large nonstick skillet coated with cooking spray, cook onion over medium heat for 2 minutes. Add shrimp; cook and stir 2-3 minutes longer. Drain.

Place crust on a pizza pan or baking sheet; spread with white sauce. Top with shrimp mixture and cheese. Bake at 425° for 8-12 minutes or until shrimp turn pink and cheese is melted. **Yield: 6 slices.**

alfredo bacon mushroom pizza

tomato spinach pizza

Prep: 1 hour / **Bake:** 20 min.

Sharlin Blamires, Coweta, Oklahoma

When you want to get your kids to eat spinach, serve it on a pizza such as this one and watch them gobble it up! A bread machine really cuts down on the prep time for the crust.

- 1-1/4 cups water (70° to 80°)
- 2 tablespoons olive oil
- 3/4 teaspoon salt
- 4 cups all-purpose flour
- 1 tablespoon active dry yeast

TOPPINGS:
- 1 tablespoon olive oil
- 3 tablespoons grated Parmesan cheese
- 1 tablespoon Italian seasoning
- 3/4 teaspoon garlic salt
- 1 package (10 ounces) frozen chopped spinach, thawed and squeezed dry
- 3 plum tomatoes, thinly sliced
- 2 cups (8 ounces) shredded part-skim mozzarella cheese

In bread machine pan, place the first five ingredients in order suggested by manufacturer. Select dough setting (check dough after 5 minutes of mixing; add 1 to 2 tablespoons of water or flour if needed).

When cycle is completed, turn dough onto a lightly floured surface. Roll into a 16-in. x 11-in. rectangle. Transfer dough to a 15-in. x 10-in. x 1-in. baking pan coated with cooking spray. Build up edges slightly. Prick dough thoroughly with a fork. Brush with oil; sprinkle with Parmesan cheese, Italian seasoning and garlic salt. Top with spinach, sliced tomatoes and shredded mozzarella cheese.

Bake at 375° for 17-22 minutes or until the crust is golden brown and the cheese is melted. Broil 4-6 in. from the heat for 2-3 minutes or until cheese is golden brown. **Yield:** 9 servings (18 slices).

alfredo bacon mushroom pizza

Prep/Total Time: 30 min.

Kami Horch, Frankfort, Maine

For a simple treat that looks and tastes like gourmet fare, look no further. Creamy Alfredo sauce complements toppings of mushroom, bacon and cheese.

- 1 loaf (1 pound) frozen pizza dough, thawed
- 1/2 pound bacon strips
- 1 cup roasted garlic Alfredo sauce
- 1-1/2 cups (6 ounces) shredded part-skim mozzarella cheese
- 1/4 cup grated Parmesan cheese
- 2 large portobello mushrooms, stems removed
- 1/4 teaspoon pepper

Roll dough into a 15-in. circle; transfer to a greased 14-in. pizza pan and build up edges slightly. Bake at 425° for 6-8 minutes or until lightly browned. Meanwhile, in a large skillet, cook bacon just until done. Drain on paper towels; cut into 1-in. pieces.

Spread Alfredo sauce over crust; sprinkle with cheeses. Cut mushrooms into 1/2-in. strips; place over cheese so they resemble spokes of a wheel. Sprinkle with bacon and pepper. Bake for 10-15 minutes or until heated through and cheese is melted. **Yield:** 8 slices.

tomato spinach pizza

chicken fajita pizza

Prep: 25 min. / **Bake:** 10 min.

Rebecca Clark, Warrior, Alabama

This South-of-the-border fare is packed with flavorful seasonings, but it's the cilantro that gives it a fresh burst of flavor. If you like Mexican food and pizza, this one is for you!

1	tube (13.8 ounces) refrigerated pizza crust
1	pound boneless skinless chicken breasts, cubed
3	teaspoons canola oil, *divided*
1	teaspoon fajita seasoning mix
1	medium sweet red pepper, julienned
1	medium green pepper, julienned
1	medium onion, halved and sliced
1	garlic clove, minced
1/2	cup salsa
1/4	teaspoon pepper
1-1/2	cups (6 ounces) shredded reduced-fat Mexican cheese blend
2	tablespoons minced fresh cilantro

Unroll crust into a 15-in. x 10-in. x 1-in. baking pan coated with cooking spray; flatten dough and build up edges slightly. Bake at 425° for 7-10 minutes or until golden brown.

Meanwhile, in a large nonstick skillet, saute the chicken in 2 teaspoons oil until no longer pink. Sprinkle with seasoning mix; cook 30 seconds longer. Remove and keep warm.

In the same skillet, saute peppers and onion in remaining oil for 3 minutes. Add garlic; cook 1 minutes longer or until vegetables are crisp-tender. Remove from the heat; stir in the salsa, pepper and reserved chicken.

Spoon the chicken mixture over crust; sprinkle with cheese. Bake for 6-10 minutes or until the cheese is melted. Sprinkle with cilantro. **Yield: 6 servings.**

pizza lover's pie

Prep: 20 min. / **Bake:** 20 min.

Carol Gillespie, Chambersburg, Pennsylvania

Love pizza? Then you'll devour this mouthwatering deep-dish, double crust pie. Plus, it's easy to tailor the toppings for the picky eaters in your household.

1/4	pound bulk pork sausage
1/2	cup chopped green pepper
1/4	cup chopped onion
1	loaf (1 pound) frozen bread dough, thawed and halved
2	cups (8 ounces) shredded part-skim mozzarella cheese
1/2	cup grated Parmesan cheese
1	can (8 ounces) pizza sauce
8	slices pepperoni
1	can (4 ounces) mushroom stems and pieces, drained
1/4	teaspoon dried oregano

In a large skillet, cook the sausage, pepper and onion over medium heat until meat is no longer pink; drain. Set aside.

Roll half of dough into a 12-in. circle. Transfer dough to a greased 9-in. deep-dish pie plate. Layer dough with half of the mozzarella cheese, Parmesan cheese and pizza sauce. Top with the sausage mixture, pepperoni, mushrooms and 1/8 teaspoon oregano.

Roll out the remaining dough to fit the top of the pie. Place over filling; seal edges. Layer with remaining pizza sauce, cheeses and oregano. Bake at 400° for 18-22 minutes or until golden brown. **Yield: 8 servings.**

pesto pizza

Prep/Total Time: 25 min.

Arlyn Kantz, Ft. Worth, Texas

This pesto-based pie is a recipe from a friend. The simplicity of the ingredients leads to a scrumptious dinner experience.

- 1/2 cup olive oil
- 4 whole garlic cloves
- 1-1/2 cups lightly packed fresh basil leaves
- 1 prebaked 12-inch pizza crust
- Shredded part-skim mozzarella cheese and toppings of your choice

In a blender, combine oil and garlic; cover and process until smooth. Add basil and blend thoroughly. Spread over crust. Sprinkle with toppings. Bake at 425° for 10 minutes. **Yield: 6-8 servings.**

smoked salmon pizza

Prep/Total Time: 25 min.

Kathy Petty, Portland, Oregon

Smoked salmon adds an upscale twist to ordinary pizza. It makes an effortless, elegant addition to your menu.

- 1 prebaked 12-inch thin pizza crust
- 1/2 cup ranch salad dressing
- 6 slices tomato
- 1/2 cup crumbled feta cheese
- 1 package (3 ounces) smoked salmon *or* lox
- 4 slices provolone cheese, cut in half

Place crust on an ungreased 14-in. pizza pan. Spread with ranch dressing; top with tomato, feta cheese and salmon. Arrange provolone cheese over top. Bake at 425° for 15-20 minutes or until cheese is melted. **Yield: 6-8 slices.**

barbecued chicken pizza

Prep/Total Time: 20 min.

Patricia Richardson, Verona, Ontario

Barbecue sauce replaces tomato sauce in this deliciously different entree. A prebaked crust makes this dinner a snap.

- 1 prebaked 12-inch pizza crust
- 2/3 cup honey garlic barbecue sauce
- 1 small red onion, chopped
- 1 cup cubed cooked chicken
- 2 cups (8 ounces) shredded part-skim mozzarella cheese

Place the crust on a 14-in. pizza pan. Spread barbecue sauce to within 1/2 in. of edges. Sprinkle with onion, chicken and cheese. Bake at 350° for 10 minutes or until cheese is melted. **Yield: 4 servings.**

rustic vegetarian pizza

rustic vegetarian pizza

Prep: 20 min. / **Bake:** 30 min. + standing

Priscilla Gilbert, Indian Harbour Beach, Florida

While my husband was stationed in Naples, Italy, we tried all kinds of pizzas with fresh ingredients. This veggie version is delish, and surprisingly simple.

- 1 tablespoon cornmeal
- 1 tube (13.8 ounces) refrigerated pizza crust
- 1-1/2 teaspoons olive oil, *divided*
- 11 slices part-skim mozzarella cheese, *divided*
- 1 small zucchini, cut into 1/8-inch slices, patted dry, *divided*
- 1 small onion, sliced
- 4 plum tomatoes, cut into 1/4-inch slices
- 1/4 teaspoon salt
- 1/4 teaspoon pepper
- 1/4 cup torn fresh basil

Sprinkle cornmeal over a greased baking sheet. Unroll pizza crust; shape into a 12-in. square. Place on the baking sheet. Brush with 1 teaspoon oil. Arrange nine slices of cheese over dough to within 1 in. of edges. Cut each remaining cheese slice into four pieces; set aside.

Place half of the zucchini, about 2 in. apart, around edges of cheese. Fold edges of dough about 1 in. over zucchini. Bake at 400° for 6 minutes. Layer with onion and remaining zucchini; top with tomatoes. Sprinkle with salt and pepper. Bake for 16 minutes or until crust is golden brown.

Arrange reserved cheese over the tomatoes; bake 4 minutes longer or until cheese is melted. Drizzle with remaining oil. Sprinkle with basil. Let stand for 10 minutes before slicing. **Yield: 4-6 servings.**

spinach stuffed pizza

Prep: 20 min. + rising / **Bake:** 30 min.

Nancy Gilmour, Sumner, Iowa

I had my first stuffed pizza when I attended college near Chicago. I was amazed to see pizza well over an inch thick, with toppings on the inside! When I served this version at home, there weren't any leftovers.

- 1 loaf (1 pound) frozen bread dough, thawed
- 1 package (10 ounces) frozen chopped spinach, thawed and squeezed dry
- 1 cup chopped fresh mushrooms
- 1/2 cup chopped onion
- 1/4 teaspoon salt
- 1/8 teaspoon pepper
- 2 cups (8 ounces) shredded part-skim mozzarella cheese
- 1/2 cup pizza sauce
- 2 tablespoons shredded Parmesan cheese

Place dough in a greased bowl, turning once to grease top. Cover and let rise in a warm place until doubled, about 1 hour. Punch dough down; divide into thirds.

On a lightly floured surface, roll one portion of dough into a 10-in. circle. Transfer to a 9-in. springform pan coated with cooking spray. Press the dough onto the bottom and up the sides of pan.

In a large bowl, combine the spinach, mushrooms, onion, salt and pepper. Sprinkle half of the shredded mozzarella cheese over crust. Cover cheese with spinach mixture; sprinkle with remaining mozzarella.

On a lightly floured surface, roll out a second portion of dough into a 10-in. circle; place over cheese layer. Pinch together top and bottom crust. (Save remaining dough for another use).

Bake at 400° for 25-30 minutes or until lightly browned. Spread pizza sauce over top crust; sprinkle with Parmesan cheese. Bake 5-6 minutes longer or until cheese is melted. Let stand for 5 minutes before cutting. **Yield: 6 servings.**

spinach stuffed pizza

turkey pizza

turkey pizza

Prep: 15 min. / **Bake:** 25 min.

Taste of Home Test Kitchen

You'll never order a delivered pizza again after diving into this irresistible "homemade" version. Refrigerated pizza crust is topped with turkey sausage, artichoke hearts and cheese.

- 1 package (20 ounces) turkey Italian sausage links
- 1 teaspoon olive oil
- 2 tubes (13.8 ounces *each*) refrigerated pizza crust
- 1 can (15 ounces) pizza sauce
- 1 cup sliced red onion
- 1 can (14 ounces) water-packed artichoke hearts, rinsed, drained and chopped
- 2 large tomatoes, sliced
- 2 cups (8 ounces) shredded Italian cheese blend

In a large skillet, cook sausage in oil over medium heat for 8-10 minutes or until no longer pink. Cut into 1/4-in. slices.

Press pizza dough into a greased 15-in. x 10-in. x 1-in. baking pan, building up edges slightly; seal seam. Prick the dough thoroughly with a fork. Bake at 400° for 8 minutes or until crust is lightly browned.

Spread with pizza sauce; top with sausage, onion, artichokes and tomatoes. Sprinkle with cheese. Bake for 15-20 minutes or until crust is golden brown. **Yield: 8 servings.**

two-meat pizza

Prep: 30 min. / **Bake:** 25 min.

Kathy Mulville, Sterling Heights, Michigan

I make this tasty, from-scratch specialty for family birthday parties. It has a thick, chewy crust and hearty toppings.

CRUST:

1	package (1/4 ounce) active dry yeast
1-1/2	cups warm water (110° to 115°)
2	tablespoons canola oil
1-1/4	cups whole wheat flour
2	tablespoons sugar
1/2	teaspoon salt
1-3/4 to 2	cups all-purpose flour

TOPPINGS:

1	can (15 ounces) pizza sauce
1	teaspoon sugar
1/2	cup sliced mushrooms
1/4	cup chopped onion
1/4	cup sliced ripe olives
1/2	pound bulk Italian sausage, cooked and drained
4	ounces Canadian bacon, chopped
2	cups (8 ounces) shredded part-skim mozzarella cheese

In a large bowl, dissolve yeast in water; add oil. Combine whole wheat flour, sugar and salt; add to yeast mixture. Stir until smooth. Stir in enough flour to form a soft dough.

Turn onto a floured surface; knead until smooth and elastic, about 6-8 minutes. Place in a greased bowl; turn once to grease top. Cover; let rise in a warm place for 15-20 minutes. Punch dough down. Pat dough onto the bottom and 1 in. up the sides of a greased 14-in. pizza pan.

Combine sauce and sugar; spread over crust. Sprinkle with mushrooms, onion and olives. Layer with sausage, Canadian bacon and cheese. Bake at 350° for 25-30 minutes or until cheese is melted. **Yield: 8 slices.**

two-meat pizza

bacon, lettuce & tomato pizza pie

bacon, lettuce & tomato pizza pie

Prep/Total Time: 25 min.

Marilyn Ruggles, Lees Summit, Missouri

A prebaked crust and all the traditional BLT sandwich fixings form this unique and much-loved pie. My hungry family gladly gobbles up slices in a hurry. Try it the next time you want a break from the usual.

1	prebaked 12-inch pizza crust
1/2	cup Miracle Whip
2	teaspoons dried basil
1/2	teaspoon garlic powder
1/8	teaspoon onion powder
12	bacon strips, cooked and crumbled
3/4	cup shredded cheddar cheese
3/4	cup shredded part-skim mozzarella cheese
1-1/2	cups shredded lettuce
2	medium tomatoes, thinly sliced

Place the prebaked pizza crust on an ungreased 12-in. pizza pan. In a small bowl, combine the Miracle Whip, basil, garlic powder and onion powder; spread Miracle Whip mixture over pizza crust.

Set aside 1/4 cup crumbled bacon. Sprinkle shredded cheddar and mozzarella cheeses and remaining bacon over crust.

Bake at 425° for 8-12 minutes or until the crust is golden and cheese is melted. Top pizza with shredded lettuce, sliced tomatoes and reserved bacon. Cut pizza into wedges. **Yield: 4-6 servings.**

italian cream cake / page 105

103

102

Indulge in this tasty assortment of "dolce Italiano."
From luscious gelato and rich, decadent cheesecakes to flaky pastries and smooth coffee beverages, these sweet offerings will both impress and delight.

cannoli cupcakes 98
lemon gelato 98
espresso panna cotta 99
easy tiramisu 99
cannoli cheesecake 99
italian cookies 100
morning latte 100
mascarpone cheesecake 101
chocolate cannoli cake 102
lemon ricotta cheesecake 102
easy espresso 103
cannoli pudding 103
sicilian fig pastries 103
tiramisu 104
pizzelle 104
spumoni slices 104
italian cream cake 105
italian lemon frozen dessert 105
tiramisu parfaits 106
tender italian sugar cookies 106
genoise with fruit 'n' cream filling 107
lemon 'n' lime strawberry ice 107

cannoli cupcakes

Prep: 50 min. / **Bake:** 25 min. + cooling

Taste of Home Test Kitchen

These jumbo cupcakes from our home economists feature a fluffy, creamy cannoli-like filling. Whimsical white chocolate curls on top are the crowning touch.

1	package (18-1/4 ounces) white cake mix
3/4	cup heavy whipping cream, *divided*
1	cup ricotta cheese
1	cup confectioners' sugar
1/2	cup Mascarpone cheese
1/4	teaspoon almond extract
1/2	cup chopped pistachios
4	ounces white baking chocolate, chopped

White chocolate curls

Prepare cake mix batter according to package directions. Fill paper-lined jumbo muffin cups three-fourths full. Bake according to package directions for 24-28 minutes or until a toothpick inserted near the center comes out clean. Cool for 10 minutes before removing from pans to wire racks to cool completely.

In a small bowl, beat 1/2 cup cream until stiff peaks form; set aside. In a large bowl, combine the ricotta cheese, confectioner's sugar, Mascarpone cheese and extract until smooth. Fold in pistachios and reserved whipped cream.

Cut the top off of each cupcake. Spread or pipe cupcakes with cheese mixture; replace tops. In a small saucepan, melt white baking chocolate with remaining cream over low heat;

stir until smooth. Remove from the heat. Cool to room temperature. Spoon over cupcakes; sprinkle with chocolate curls. Refrigerate leftovers. **Yield: 8 cupcakes.**

lemon gelato

Prep: 30 min. / **Process:** 20 min./batch + freezing

Gail Wang, Troy, Michigan

On a trip to Italy, I fell in love with gelato. My top choice was lemon because of the intense, refreshing flavor. This homemade recipe brings back memories of our vacation.

1	cup milk
1	cup sugar
5	egg yolks, lightly beaten
3	tablespoons grated lemon peel
3/4	cup lemon juice
2	cups heavy whipping cream

In a small heavy saucepan, heat milk to 175°; stir in sugar until dissolved. Whisk a small amount of hot mixture into egg yolks. Return all to the pan, whisking constantly. Add lemon peel. Cook and stir over low heat until mixture reaches at least 160° and coats the back of a metal spoon.

Remove from the heat; strain. Stir in lemon juice. Cool quickly by placing pan in a bowl of ice water; stir for 2 minutes. Stir in cream. Cover and refrigerate for several hours or overnight.

Fill the cylinder of an ice cream freezer two-thirds full; freeze according to manufacturer's directions. Refrigerate remaining mixture until ready to freeze. Transfer to a freezer container; freeze for 2-4 hours before serving. **Yield: 1-1/2 quarts.**

lemon gelato

espresso panna cotta

Prep: 15 min. / **Cook:** 10 min. + chilling

Nicole Clayton, Prescott, Arizona

I got this fun presentation idea after seeing similar desserts at various restaurants. The martini glasses make an elegant impression for such a sweet treat. Best of all, guests can easily mingle while carrying the panna cotta.

- 1   envelope unflavored gelatin
- 1   cup milk
- 3   cups heavy whipping cream
- 1/2   cup sugar
- 2   tablespoons instant espresso powder *or* instant coffee granules
- 1/8   teaspoon salt

Dark and white chocolate curls

In a small saucepan, sprinkle gelatin over milk; let stand for 1 minute. Heat over low heat, stirring until the gelatin is completely dissolved. Stir in the cream, sugar, espresso powder and salt. Cook and stir until the sugar is dissolved. Remove from the heat. Pour into six dessert dishes. Cover and refrigerate for 1 hour, stirring every 20 minutes. Refrigerate for at least 5 hours longer or until set. Just before serving, garnish with chocolate curls. **Yield: 6 servings.**

easy tiramisu

Prep/Total Time: 20 min.

Nancy Brown, Dahinda, Illinois

If you love tiramisu, but not the preparation that goes into it, try this simpler version. It takes just moments to prepare without sacrificing any of the luscious decadence.

- 1   package (10-3/4 ounces) frozen pound cake, thawed
- 3/4   cup strong brewed coffee
- 1   package (8 ounces) cream cheese, softened
- 1   cup sugar
- 1/2   cup chocolate syrup

- 1   cup heavy whipping cream, whipped
- 2   Heath candy bars (1.4 ounces *each*), crushed

Cut cake into nine slices. Arrange in an ungreased 11-in. x 7-in. dish, cutting to fit if needed. Drizzle with coffee.

In a small bowl, beat cream cheese and sugar until smooth. Add chocolate syrup. Fold in whipped cream. Spread over cake. Sprinkle with crushed candy bars. Refrigerate tiramisu until serving. **Yield: 8 servings.**

cannoli cheesecake

Prep: 25 min. / **Bake:** 1 hour 5 minutes + chilling

Marie McConnell, Las Cruces, New Mexico

This finale combines two of our favorite desserts—cannoli and cheesecake. It's become a family tradition at holiday parties.

- 3   cartons (15 ounces *each*) ricotta cheese
- 1-1/2   cups sugar
- 1/2   cup all-purpose flour
- 3   teaspoons vanilla extract
- 2   teaspoons grated orange peel
- 7   eggs, lightly beaten
- 1/3   cup miniature semisweet chocolate chips
- 1/4   cup chopped pistachios

Place a greased 9-in. springform pan on a double thickness of heavy-duty foil (about 18 in. square). Securely wrap foil around pan; set aside.

In a large bowl, beat ricotta cheese and sugar until blended. Beat in the flour, vanilla and orange peel. Add eggs; beat on low speed just until combined. Pour into prepared pan; sprinkle with chocolate chips. Place in a large baking pan; add 1 in. of hot water to larger pan.

Bake at 350° for 65-75 minutes or until center is almost set. Remove pan from water bath. Cool on a wire rack for 10 minutes. Carefully run a knife around edge of pan to loosen; cool 1 hour longer. Refrigerate overnight. Sprinkle with pistachios. **Yield: 12 servings.**

italian cookies

Prep: 20 min. **/ Bake:** 10 min./batch

Marie Forte, Raritan, New Jersey

My 100% Italian husband will tell you these are his favorite cookies. I make them often and definitely every Christmas. They're good with or without icing, coconut and sprinkles.

- 1/2 pound butter, softened
- 1/2 cup sugar
- 6 eggs
- 2 teaspoons vanilla *or* anise extract
- 4 cups all-purpose flour
- 4 teaspoons baking powder

ICING:

- 3-3/4 cups confectioners' sugar
- 5 to 6 tablespoons milk
- 2 teaspoons vanilla extract

DECORATIONS:

Flaked coconut *or* assorted sprinkles

In a large bowl, cream butter and sugar until light and fluffy. Beat in eggs and extract. Combine flour and baking powder; gradually add to creamed mixture and mix well.

Drop by rounded teaspoonfuls onto ungreased baking sheets. Bake at 350° for 9-11 minutes or until bottoms are lightly browned. Remove to wire racks to cool completely.

For icing, in a small bowl, combine the confectioners' sugar, milk and vanilla until smooth. Dip cookies, allowing excess to drip off. Place on waxed paper; decorate as desired. Let stand until set. **Yield: 7 dozen.**

italian cookies

morning latte

morning latte

Prep/Total Time: 10 min.

Taste of Home Test Kitchen

A latte has the same ingredients as a cappuccino, but it is topped with just a thin layer of foamy milk. This recipe results in a classic coffee concoction as rich and pleasing as any you would find at a pricey coffeehouse.

- 1/2 cup milk
- 1/3 cup hot brewed Easy Espresso (see page 103)

Place the milk in a 1-cup microwave-safe measuring cup. Microwave, uncovered, on high for 1 minute or until milk is hot and small bubbles form around edge of cup.

Place a metal whisk in cup; whisk vigorously by holding whisk handle loosely between palms and quickly rubbing hands back and forth. Remove foam to a small measuring cup as it forms. Continue whisking until foam measures 1/8 to 1/4 cup; set aside.

Pour Easy Espresso into a cup; pour in remaining hot milk. Spoon the foam over top of espresso and serve immediately. **Yield: 1 serving.**

Editor's Note: You may also use a portable mixer with whisk attachment to froth the milk.

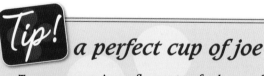

Tip! *a perfect cup of joe*

To preserve maximum flavor, store fresh ground or whole bean coffee in an airtight container in the refrigerator for up to 2 weeks. For the best-tasting coffee, always start with a clean coffee maker and brew coffee with fresh cold water.

mascarpone cheesecake

Prep: 30 min. / **Bake:** 50 min. + chilling

Deanna Polito-Laughinghouse, Raleigh, North Carolina

This scrumptious dessert is sure to delight with its creamy filling, whipped topping and sweet caramel drizzle. A luscious cheesecake such as this makes an ideal ending to an Italian feast.

- 3/4 cup graham cracker crumbs
- 3 tablespoons sugar
- 3 tablespoons butter, melted

FILLING:

- 2 packages (8 ounces *each*) cream cheese, softened
- 2 cartons (8 ounces *each*) Mascarpone cheese
- 1 cup sugar
- 1 tablespoon lemon juice
- 1 tablespoon vanilla extract
- 4 eggs, lightly beaten

TOPPING:

- 1 envelope whipped topping mix (Dream Whip)
- 1 tablespoon caramel ice cream topping

Place a greased 9-in. springform pan on a double thickness of heavy-duty foil (about 18 in. square). Securely wrap foil around pan.

In a small bowl, combine graham cracker crumbs and sugar; stir in butter. Press onto the bottom of prepared pan. Place pan on a baking sheet. Bake at 325° for 10 minutes. Cool on a wire rack.

For filling, in a large bowl, beat the cheeses, sugar, lemon juice and vanilla until smooth. Add eggs; beat on low speed just until combined. Pour over crust. Place springform pan in a large baking pan; add 1 in. of hot water to larger pan.

Bake at 325° for 50-60 minutes or until center is just set and top appears dull. Remove springform pan from water bath. Cool on a wire rack for 10 minutes. Carefully run a knife around the edge of pan to loosen; cool 1 hour longer.

Refrigerate cheesecake overnight. Before serving, prepare the topping mix according to package directions. Garnish cheesecake with whipped topping; drizzle with caramel ice cream topping. Refrigerate leftovers. **Yield: 12 servings.**

chocolate cannoli cake

chocolate cannoli cake

Prep: 25 min. / **Bake:** 25 min. + cooling

Mary Bilyeu, Ann Arbor, Michigan

Subtle hints of orange and coffee lend standout flavor to every bite of this decadent cake. A variation of this rich dessert was a finalist in a local baking contest.

- 1 egg white, lightly beaten
- 1 cup reduced-fat ricotta cheese
- 1/4 cup sugar
- 1 tablespoon cold brewed coffee
- 2 teaspoons grated orange peel
- 1/2 cup miniature semisweet chocolate chips

BATTER:
- 1 cup sugar
- 1/2 cup cold brewed coffee
- 1/3 cup canola oil
- 1/3 cup orange juice
- 1 egg
- 1 egg white
- 1 tablespoon cider vinegar
- 1 tablespoon vanilla extract
- 1 cup all-purpose flour
- 1/2 cup whole wheat flour
- 1/3 cup baking cocoa
- 2 teaspoons baking powder
- 1/2 teaspoon salt

In a small bowl, combine the egg white, ricotta cheese, sugar, coffee and orange peel. Stir in chocolate chips; set aside.

In a large bowl, combine the first eight batter ingredients; beat until well blended. Combine the all-purpose flour, whole wheat flour, cocoa, baking powder and salt; gradually beat into sugar mixture until blended.

Transfer to a 13-in. x 9-in. baking dish coated with cooking spray. Top with heaping tablespoons of ricotta mixture; cut through batter with a knife to swirl. Bake at 350° for 25-30 minutes or until a toothpick inserted near the center comes out clean. Cool on a wire rack. Refrigerate leftovers. **Yield: 15 servings.**

lemon ricotta cheesecake

Prep: 35 min. / **Bake:** 70 min. + chilling

Julie Nitschke, Stowe, Vermont

I'm an avid recipe collector and can't recall where I found this one. But I do know its delicate lemon zing is always well received when I make it for special-occasion dinners.

- 1-1/2 cups crushed vanilla wafers (about 45 wafers)
- 1/4 cup butter, melted
- 1 teaspoon grated lemon peel

FILLING:
- 2 packages (8 ounces *each*) cream cheese, softened
- 1 carton (15 ounces) ricotta cheese
- 1-1/4 cups sugar
- 1/4 cup cornstarch
- 4 eggs
- 2 cups half-and-half cream
- 1/3 cup lemon juice
- 3 teaspoons grated lemon peel
- 2 teaspoons vanilla extract

Fresh mint and lemon slices, optional

In a small bowl, combine wafer crumbs, butter and lemon peel. Press onto the bottom of a greased 9-in. springform pan. Bake at 325° for 12-14 minutes or until lightly browned. Let crust cool.

In a large bowl, beat cream cheese and ricotta until smooth. Combine sugar and cornstarch; add to cheese mixture and beat well. Add eggs and cream, beating on low speed just until combined. Beat in lemon juice, peel and vanilla until blended. Pour into crust. Place pan on a baking sheet.

Bake at 325° for 70-80 minutes or until center is almost set. Cool on a wire rack for 10 minutes. Carefully run a knife around edge of pan to loosen; cool 1 hour longer. Refrigerate overnight. Garnish with fresh mint and lemon if desired. **Yield: 12-14 servings.**

lemon ricotta cheesecake

easy espresso

Prep/Total Time: 10 min.

Taste of Home Test Kitchen

Capture the classic taste of coffeehouse espresso without the hassle of expensive brewing equipment! For best flavor, serve the espresso immediately. Our home economists suggest pouring any leftover beverage in ice cube trays and freezing it to use later in cold drinks.

1/2	cup ground coffee (French or other dark roast)
1-1/2	cups cold water
	Lemon twists, optional

Place ground coffee in the filter of a drip coffeemaker. Add water; brew according to manufacturer's instructions. Serve immediately in espresso cups with lemon twists if desired. **Yield: 4 servings.**

Editor's Note: This recipe was tested with Starbucks French Roast ground coffee.

cannoli pudding

Prep/Total Time: 10 min.

Kat Thompson, Prineville, Oregon

This subtly sweet and creamy pudding lets you enjoy the appeal of a traditional Italian dessert in a fraction of the time.

1	carton (15 ounces) ricotta cheese
1/4	cup miniature semisweet chocolate chips
1/4	cup chopped pecans
1/4	cup chopped maraschino cherries
3	tablespoons sugar
3	tablespoons heavy whipping cream
	Whole maraschino cherries, optional

In a large bowl, beat ricotta cheese until smooth. Stir in the chocolate chips, pecans, cherries, sugar and cream. Spoon into dessert dishes. Refrigerate until serving. Garnish with whole cherries if desired. **Yield: 4 servings.**

sicilian fig pastries

Prep: 45 min. / **Bake:** 15 min./batch

Weda Mosellie, Phillipsburg, New Jersey

These fig-filled desserts have true European flair. They add just the right amount of sweetness to the dessert tray.

4	cups all-purpose flour
3/4	cup shortening
1/4	teaspoon salt
1/3	cup sugar
1/2	cup warm water
1	egg, lightly beaten
1/4	teaspoon vanilla extract

FILLING:

8	ounces dried figs, chopped
2/3	cup chopped walnuts
1	tablespoon water
1	tablespoon grape jelly
1/2	teaspoon grated orange peel
1/8	teaspoon ground cinnamon
1	egg, lightly beaten
2	tablespoons sugar

In a food processor, combine the flour, shortening and salt; cover and process until mixture resembles coarse crumbs. In a small bowl, dissolve sugar in warm water; stir in egg and vanilla. Gradually add to crumb mixture; pulse until dough forms a ball. Cover and let rest for 10 minutes.

In a food processor, combine the figs, walnuts, water, grape jelly, orange peel and cinnamon; cover and process until blended. Set aside.

Separate dough into six portions. On a lightly floured surface, roll each portion into a 12-in. x 8-in. rectangle (dough will be very thin). Cut into 4-in. x 2-in. rectangles. Place a teaspoon of fig mixture on one short side of each rectangle; fold dough over filling. Press edges with a fork to seal. Place 1 in. apart on ungreased baking sheets. Brush with egg and sprinkle with sugar. Bake at 375° for 15-17 minutes or until golden brown. Remove from pans to wire racks. **Yield: 3 dozen.**

sicilian fig pastries

tiramisu

Prep/Total Time: 20 min. + chilling

Taste of Home Test Kitchen

No one can resist this classic, creamy after-dinner delight created by our home economists. The no-fuss version is quick to prepare and can be made ahead for added convenience.

- 2 cups cold milk
- 1 package (3.4 ounces) instant vanilla pudding mix
- 1 cup heavy whipping cream
- 3 tablespoons confectioners' sugar
- 18 ladyfingers, split
- 2-1/2 teaspoons instant coffee granules
- 1/2 cup boiling water
- 1 tablespoon baking cocoa

In a large bowl, whisk milk and pudding mix for 2 minutes. Let stand for 2 minutes or until soft-set. In a small bowl, beat cream until it begins to thicken. Add confectioners' sugar; beat until soft peaks form. Fold into pudding; cover and refrigerate.

Arrange half of the ladyfingers cut side up in an 11-in. x 7-in. dish. Dissolve coffee granules in boiling water; drizzle half over the ladyfingers. Spread with half of the pudding mixture. Repeat layers. Sprinkle with cocoa. Refrigerate until serving. **Yield: 6 servings.**

tiramisu

pizzelle

Prep: 10 min. / **Cook:** 5 min./batch

Elizabeth Schwartz, Trevorton, Pennsylvania

This recipe was adapted from one used by my Italian-born mother and grandmother. They used old irons on a gas stove, but now we have the convenience of electric pizzelle irons.

- 18 eggs
- 3-1/2 cups sugar
- 1-1/4 cups canola oil
- 1 tablespoon anise oil
- 6-1/2 cups all-purpose flour

In a large bowl, beat the eggs, sugar and oils until smooth. Gradually add flour and mix well. Bake in a preheated pizzelle iron according to manufacturer's directions until golden brown. Remove to wire racks to cool. Store in an airtight container. **Yield: 7 dozen.**

spumoni slices

Prep: 40 min. + chilling / **Bake:** 10 min./batch

Mary Chupp, Chattanooga, Tennessee

These irresistible treats get their name from the old-fashioned, tri-colored ice cream. This is our family's dessert of choice.

- 1 cup butter, softened
- 1-1/2 cups confectioners' sugar
- 1 egg
- 1 teaspoon vanilla extract
- 2-1/2 cups all-purpose flour
- 2 ounces semisweet chocolate, melted
- 1/2 cup chopped pecans
- 3 to 5 drops green food coloring
- 1/4 cup finely chopped candied red cherries
- 1/2 teaspoon almond extract
- 3 to 5 drops red food coloring

In a large bowl, cream butter and sugar until light and fluffy. Beat in egg and vanilla. Gradually add flour and mix well. Divide dough in three portions. Stir chocolate into one portion. Add pecans and green food coloring to the second portion. Add cherries, almond extract and red food coloring to the third.

Roll each portion between two pieces of waxed paper into an 8-in. x 6-in. rectangle. Remove waxed paper. Place chocolate rectangle on a piece of plastic wrap. Top with the green and pink rectangles; press together lightly. Wrap with plastic wrap and chill overnight.

Cut chilled dough in half lengthwise. Return one rectangle to the refrigerator. Cut remaining rectangle into 1/8-in. slices. Place 1 in. apart on ungreased baking sheets. Bake at 375° for 5-7 minutes or until set. Cool for 2 minutes before removing to wire racks. Repeat with remaining dough. **Yield: about 7 dozen.**

italian cream cake

near the center comes out clean. Cool for 10 minutes before removing from pans to wire racks to cool completely.

For frosting, in a large bowl, beat cream cheese and butter until fluffy. Add confectioners' sugar and vanilla; beat until smooth. Spread frosting between layers and over top and sides of cake. Press pecans onto sides of cake. Store in the refrigerator. **Yield: 12 servings.**

italian lemon frosted dessert

Prep: 20 min. + cooling / **Cook:** 20 min. + freezing

Sally Sibthorpe, Shelby Township, Michigan

Lemon fans will devour this refreshing summer sensation. Consider garnishing individual servings with fresh berries.

```
5     eggs
1     cup sugar
1     cup ricotta cheese
1/2   cup plus 3 tablespoons butter, melted,
      divided
1     cup lemon juice
1     tablespoon grated lemon peel
1-1/2 cups heavy whipping cream
1     cup amaretti cookie crumbs
```

In a large bowl, beat the eggs, sugar and ricotta cheese; slowly add 1/2 cup butter. Stir in lemon juice and peel. Transfer to a large saucepan. Cook and stir over medium heat until mixture reaches at least 160° and coats the back of a metal spoon. Transfer to a large bowl; cool completely.

Line a 9-in. x 5-in. loaf pan with plastic wrap. In a small bowl, whip the cream until soft peaks form. Fold into cooled lemon mixture. Pour into prepared pan. Combine cookie crumbs and remaining butter; sprinkle over lemon mixture. Cover and freeze for several hours or overnight.

Remove 10 minutes before serving. Using plastic wrap, lift dessert out of pan. Invert onto a serving platter; discard the plastic wrap. Cut into slices. **Yield: 8 servings.**

italian lemon frozen dessert

italian cream cake

Prep: 40 min. / **Bake:** 20 min. + cooling

Marilyn Morel, Keene, New Hampshire

Here's a jaw-dropping finale that melts in your mouth and makes you say, "Mil a Grazi!" (That means "Thanks a million!") Pecan lovers will eagerly accept a second slice of this buttery, rich and moist cake.

```
1/2   cup butter, softened
1/2   cup shortening
2     cups sugar
5     eggs
1     teaspoon vanilla extract
2     cups all-purpose flour
1     teaspoon baking soda
1/4   teaspoon salt
1     cup buttermilk
1     cup chopped pecans
1/2   cup flaked coconut
```
CREAM CHEESE FROSTING:
```
2     packages (one 8 ounces, one 3 ounces)
      cream cheese, softened
1/2   cup butter, softened
3-3/4 cups confectioners' sugar
1     teaspoon vanilla extract
1     cup coarsely chopped pecans
```

In a large bowl, cream the butter, shortening and sugar until light and fluffy. Add eggs, one at a time, beating well after each addition. Beat in vanilla. Combine the flour, baking soda and salt; add dry ingredients to creamed mixture alternately with buttermilk, beating well after each addition. Fold in chopped pecans and flaked coconut.

Pour into three greased and floured 9-in. round baking pans. Bake at 350° for 20-25 minutes or until a toothpick inserted

tiramisu parfaits

Prep/Total Time: 40 min. + chilling

Nancy Granaman, Burlington, Iowa

As a mouthwatering finale, I whip up my tiramisu and serve it in pretty parfait glasses. This is a longtime favorite tradition with my family. I think the parfaits look stunning with a drizzle of chocolate or cocoa sprinkled on top.

4-1/2	teaspoons instant coffee granules
1/3	cup boiling water
2	cups cold fat-free milk
2	packages (1 ounce *each*) sugar-free instant vanilla pudding mix
4	ounces fat-free cream cheese
1	package (3 ounces) ladyfingers, split and cubed
2	cups fat-free whipped topping
2	tablespoons miniature chocolate chips
1	teaspoon baking cocoa

Dissolve coffee in boiling water; cool to room temperature. In a large bowl, whisk milk and pudding mixes for 2 minutes. Let stand for 2 minutes or until soft-set. In another large bowl, beat cream cheese until smooth. Gradually fold in pudding.

Place ladyfinger cubes in a bowl; add coffee; toss to coat. Let ladyfingers stand for 5 minutes.

Divide half of the ladyfinger cubes among six parfait glasses or serving dishes. Top ladyfingers with half of the pudding mixture, 1 cup whipped topping and 1 tablespoon chocolate chips. Repeat the layers.

Cover and refrigerate for 8 hours or overnight. Just before serving, dust with cocoa. **Yield: 6 servings.**

tender italian sugar cookies

Prep: 20 min. / **Bake:** 10 min./batch + cooling

Weda Mosellie, Phillipsburg, New Jersey

These classic cookies are moist and a favorite of all who try them. To tie into the colors of the Italian flag, you could tint the icing, red, green and white.

3/4	cup shortening
3/4	cup sugar
3	eggs
1	teaspoon vanilla extract
3	cups all-purpose flour
3	teaspoons baking powder
1/8	teaspoon salt

ICING:

1/4	cup milk
2	tablespoons butter, melted
1/2	teaspoon vanilla extract
2-1/2	cups confectioners' sugar
	Food coloring and colored sugar, optional

In a large bowl, cream shortening and sugar until light and fluffy. Beat in eggs and vanilla. Combine the flour, baking powder and salt; gradually add dry ingredients to creamed mixture and mix well.

Shape dough into 1-1/2-in. balls. Place 1 in. apart on ungreased baking sheets. Bake at 400° for 8-10 minutes or until lightly browned. Remove to wire racks to cool.

For icing, in a small bowl, combine the milk, butter, vanilla and confectioners' sugar until smooth. Tint with food coloring if desired. Dip the tops of cookies in icing; allow excess to drip off. Sprinkle with colored sugar if desired. Place on waxed paper; let stand until set. **Yield: 3 dozen.**

tender italian sugar cookies

genoise with fruit 'n' cream filling

genoise with fruit 'n' cream filling

Prep: 35 min. / **Bake:** 25 min. + cooling

Taste of Home Test Kitchen

Sweet syrup soaks into the tender layers of his delicate sponge cake. Complete the presentation with sweetened cream and assorted fresh berries for a finale that wows.

        6   eggs, lightly beaten
        1   cup sugar
        1   teaspoon grated lemon peel
        1   teaspoon lemon extract
        1   cup all-purpose flour
      1/2   cup butter, melted and cooled
    SUGAR SYRUP:
        3   tablespoons boiling water
        2   tablespoons sugar
      1/4   cup cold water
    1-1/2   teaspoons lemon extract
    FILLING:
        1   cup heavy whipping cream
      1/2   cup confectioners' sugar
        1   teaspoon vanilla extract, optional
        3   cups mixed fresh berries

Line two greased 9-in. round baking pans with waxed paper and grease the paper; set aside. In a large heatproof bowl, combine eggs and sugar; place over a large saucepan filled with 1-2 in. of simmering water. Heat egg mixture over low heat, stirring occasionally, until the mixture reaches 110°, about 8-10 minutes.

Remove from the heat; add lemon peel and extract. With a hand mixer, beat on high speed until mixture is lemon-colored and more than doubles in volume. Fold in flour, 1/4 cup at a time. Gently fold in butter. Spread into prepared pans.

Bake at 350° for 25-30 minutes or until a toothpick inserted near the center comes out clean. Cool for 10 minutes before removing from pans to wire racks to cool completely.

In a small bowl, combine boiling water and sugar; stir until sugar is dissolved. Stir in cold water and extract. Using a fork, evenly poke 1/2-in.-deep holes in each cake. Spoon sugar syrup over cake surface.

In a small bowl, beat cream until it begins to thicken. Add sugar and vanilla if desired; beat until soft peaks form.

Place one cake on a serving platter; spread with half of the whipped cream and top with half of the berries. Repeat layers. Store in the refrigerator. **Yield: 10-12 servings.**

lemon 'n' lime strawberry ice

Prep/Total Time: 30 min. + freezing

Marie Rizzio, Interlochen, Michigan

This slushy, fruity dessert is perfect for summer. Its light citrus-and-berry flavor is so refreshing after dinner.

        1   cup sugar
      3/4   cup water
        1   tablespoon shredded orange peel
        2   teaspoons shredded lemon peel
    1-1/2   teaspoons shredded lime peel
      1/3   cup orange juice
        3   tablespoons lemon juice
        2   tablespoons lime juice
        4   cups sliced fresh strawberries

In a small saucepan, combine the first five ingredients. Bring to a boil. Reduce heat; simmer, uncovered, for 5-6 minutes or until slightly thickened. Strain; discard peels. Add juices to the syrup; cool slightly.

Place half of the juice mixture and strawberries in a blender; cover and pulse until nearly smooth. Transfer to a 2-qt. freezer container. Repeat with remaining juice mixture and berries. Cover; freeze for 12 hours or overnight, stirring several times. Ice may be frozen for up to 3 months. Just before serving, break apart with a large spoon. **Yield: 6 servings.**

lemon 'n' lime strawberry ice

general index

appetizers
Cold Appetizers
Antipasto-Stuffed Baguettes, 7
Cilantro Tomato Bruschetta, 12
Classic Antipasto Platter, 11
Pesto Chicken, 7
Prosciutto Bundles, 12
Dips & Spreads
Herb Mix for Dipping Oil, 13
Pesto Swirled Cheesecake, 11
Pizza Dip, 8
Hot Appetizers
Calzone Pinwheels, 10
Cheesy Mushroom Morsels, 9
Fried Cheese Ravioli, 13
Italian Sausage-Stuffed
    Mushrooms, 13
Rosemary Cheese Patties, 6
Rosemary Veal Meatballs, 9
Stromboli Slices, 12
Stuffed Bread Appetizers, 10
Tuscan Kabobs, 6

artichokes
Antipasto Salad with Basil
    Dressing, 33
Antipasto-Stuffed Baguettes, 7
Artichoke-Basil Pasta Sauce, 64
Monterey Artichoke Panini, 25
Rosemary Veal Meatballs, 9
Super Italian Chopped Salad, 38
Turkey Pizza, 94
Tuscan Bean Salad, 37

bacon & turkey bacon
Alfredo Bacon Mushroom Pizza, 91
Bacon, Lettuce & Tomato Pizza
    Pie, 95
Bacon-Olive Tomato Pizza, 90
Baked Potato Pizza, 90
Hearty Spaghetti Sauce, 59
Layered Tortellini Salad, 32
Pesto Tortellini Salad, 35
Tuscan Kabobs, 6
Two-Meat Pizza, 95

basil (also see Pesto)
Antipasto Medley, 34
Antipasto Salad with Basil
    Dressing, 33
Artichoke-Basil Pasta Sauce, 64
Basil-Cheese Bread Strips, 39
Blushing Penne Pasta, 67
Bruschetta Chicken, 82
Caprese Sandwiches, 22
Eggplant Parmigiana, 46
Fresh Herb Flat Bread, 28
Fresh Mozzarella Tomato Salad, 36
Herb Mix for Dipping Oil, 13
Italian Wedding Soup, 20
Linguine with Fresh Tomatoes, 71
No-Cook Herbed Tomato
    Sauce, 71
Rustic Vegetarian Pizza, 93
Shrimp and Olive Rigatoni, 79

Stromboli Slices, 12
Sweet Onion 'n' Sausage
    Spaghetti, 59
Tuscan Bean Salad, 37
Tuscan Kabobs, 6
Tuscan Tossed Salad, 39

beans
Antipasto Medley, 34
Chicken Orzo Skillet, 70
Forgotten Minestrone, 23
Pasta Fagioli Soup, 17
Super Italian Chopped Salad, 38
Tuscan Bean Salad, 37

beef (also see Ground Beef)
Forgotten Minestrone, 23
Italian Beef Sandwiches, 20
Italian Pot Roast, 83
Italian Strip Steaks with
    Focaccia, 78
Saucy Beef Roast, 81

breads & rolls
Basil-Cheese Bread Strips, 39
Easter Bread, 35
Fresh Herb Flat Bread, 28
Italian Bread, 35
Italian Bread Twists, 33
Italian Dinner Rolls, 31
Roasted Garlic Bread, 37
Tomato & Olive Bread, 32

broccoli & cauliflower
Alfredo Chicken Tortellini, 69
Antipasto Picnic Salad, 28
Broccoli Chicken Lasagna, 42
Chicken Orzo Skillet, 70
Fettuccine Primavera, 66
Garden Primavera Fettuccine, 58
Herbed Shrimp Fettuccine, 78
Italian Broccoli with Peppers, 30
Sausage Broccoli Manicotti, 51

cabbage
Forgotten Minestrone, 23
Layered Tortellini Salad, 32

cheese
Antipasto Medley, 34
Antipasto Picnic Salad, 28
Baked Ziti, 43
Basil-Cheese Bread Strips, 39
Blushing Penne Pasta, 67
Caprese Sandwiches, 22
Caramelized Onion-Gorgonzola
    Pizza, 86
Cheesy Mushroom Morsels, 9
Chicken Parmigiana, 77
Classic Antipasto Platter, 11
Eggplant Parmigiana, 46
Four-Cheese Bow Ties, 50
Fresh Mozzarella Tomato Salad, 36
Fried Cheese Ravioli, 13
Layered Tortellini Salad, 32

Lemon Ricotta Cheesecake, 102
Makeover Cheese-Stuffed
    Shells, 48
Marinated Pasta Salad, 38
Mascarpone Cheesecake, 101
Monterey Artichoke Panini, 25
Parmesan Chicken, 74
Parmesan Noodles, 60
Parmesan Red Potatoes, 36
Parmesan Romaine Salad, 31
Pepperoni Provolone Pizzas, 88
Peppy Parmesan Pasta, 62
Pesto Swirled Cheesecake, 11
Portobellos Parmesano, 36
Prosciutto Provolone Panini, 21
Red Pepper & Parmesan Tilapia, 78
Rosemary Cheese Patties, 6
Stromboli Slices, 12
Stuffed Shells Florentine, 42
Tomato Cheese Pizza, 87

chicken
Alfredo Chicken Lasagna, 45
Alfredo Chicken Tortellini, 69
Barbecued Chicken Pizza, 93
Broccoli Chicken Lasagna, 42
Bruschetta Chicken, 82
Chicken Alfredo Stromboli, 24
Chicken Cacciatore, 76
Chicken Fajita Pizza, 92
Chicken Marsala with Pasta, 79
Chicken Milan, 83
Chicken Orzo Skillet, 70
Chicken Parmigiana, 77
Chicken Pesto Pizza, 87
Chicken Piccata, 75
Chicken Spinach Manicotti, 44
Chicken Tortellini Soup, 25
Creamy Chicken Lasagna, 54
Fettuccine Primavera, 66
Florentine Chicken Soup, 22
Gnocchi Chicken Skillet, 64
Meaty Spinach Manicotti, 52
Parmesan Chicken, 74
Pesto Chicken, 7
Smothered Chicken Italiano, 81
Tuscan Chicken Soup, 21
Tuscan Kabobs, 6
Tuxedo Pasta, 65

chocolate
Cannoli Cheesecake, 99
Cannoli Pudding, 103
Chocolate Cannoli Cake, 102
Easy Tiramisu, 99
Spumoni Slices, 104
Tiramisu, 104
Tiramisu Parfaits, 106

coffee
Chocolate Cannoli Cake, 102
Easy Espresso, 103
Easy Tiramisu, 99
Espresso Panna Cotta, 99
Morning Latte, 100

Tiramisu, 104
Tiramisu Parfaits, 106

desserts
Cannoli Cheesecake, 99
Cannoli Cupcakes, 98
Cannoli Pudding, 103
Chocolate Cannoli Cake, 102
Easy Tiramisu, 99
Espresso Panna Cotta, 99
Genoise with Fruit 'n' Cream
    Filling, 107
Italian Cookies, 100
Italian Cream Cake, 105
Italian Lemon Frozen Dessert, 105
Lemon 'n' Lime Strawberry Ice, 107
Lemon Gelato, 98
Lemon Ricotta Cheesecake, 102
Mascarpone Cheesecake, 101
Pizzelle, 104
Sicilian Fig Pastries, 103
Spumoni Slices, 104
Tender Italian Sugar Cookies, 106
Tiramisu, 104
Tiramisu Parfaits, 106

eggplant
Eggplant Parmigiana, 46
Roasted Vegetable Lasagna, 48

eggs
Cannoli Cheesecake, 99
Cheesy Mushroom Morsels, 9
Classic Antipasto Platter, 11
Genoise with Fruit 'n' Cream
    Filling, 107
Italian Lemon Frozen Dessert, 105
Lemon Gelato, 98
Lemon Ricotta Cheesecake, 102
Mascarpone Cheesecake, 101
Pizzelle, 104

fish & seafood
Classic Antipasto Platter, 11
Herbed Shrimp Fettuccine, 78
Pesto Halibut, 81
Red Pepper & Parmesan Tilapia, 78
Salmon with Fettuccine Alfredo, 74
Seafood Fettuccine, 82
Shrimp and Olive Rigatoni, 79
Shrimp Pizza, 90
Smoked Salmon Pizza, 93
Tilapia Florentine, 80
Tuscan Tossed Salad, 39

fruit
Genoise with Fruit 'n' Cream
    Filling, 107
Lemon 'n' Lime Strawberry Ice, 107
Sicilian Fig Pastries, 103

garlic
Baked Potato Pizza, 90
Garlic Tomato Soup, 16
Gnocchi in Sage Butter, 68
Hearty Spaghetti Sauce, 59
No-Cook Herbed Tomato Sauce, 71
Pesto Pizza, 93
Roasted Garlic Bread, 37

grilled & broiled recipes
Barbecue Italian Sausages, 19
Salmon with Fettuccine Alfredo, 74
Tuscan Kabobs, 6

ground beef
Baked Mostaccioli, 52
Baked Ziti with Fresh Tomatoes, 55
Beef Ragu with Ravioli, 67
Cannelloni, 43
Hearty Italian Sandwiches, 18
Hearty Sausage Stromboli, 17
Hearty Spaghetti Sauce, 59
Herbed Mushroom Spaghetti
    Sauce, 66
Homemade Pizza, 86
Italian Pasta Sauce, 61
Italian Spaghetti and Meatballs, 62
Italian Spaghetti Bake, 54
Italian Stuffed Shells, 49
Italian Wedding Soup, 20
Lasagna Rolls, 46
Makeover Cheese-Stuffed Shells, 48
Meatball Calzones, 24
Ravioli Skillet, 69
Slow-Cooked Spaghetti Sauce, 63
Spaghetti Pie, 47
Spinach Meatball Subs, 23
Ziti with Roasted Red Pepper
    Sauce, 61

ham (also see Prosciutto)
Antipasto Picnic Salad, 28
Broccoli Chicken Lasagna, 42
Stuffed Bread Appetizers, 10
Super Italian Chopped Salad, 38

lemon & lime
Italian Lemon Frozen Dessert, 105
Lemon 'n' Lime Strawberry Ice, 107
Lemon Gelato, 98
Lemon Ricotta Cheesecake, 102

meatballs
Italian Spaghetti and Meatballs, 62
Meatball Calzones, 24
Rosemary Veal Meatballs, 9
Spinach Meatball Subs, 23

mushrooms
Alfredo Bacon Mushroom Pizza, 91
Alfredo Chicken Lasagna, 45
Artichoke-Basil Pasta Sauce, 64
Broccoli Chicken Lasagna, 42
Calzone Pinwheels, 10
Cheesy Mushroom Morsels, 9
Chicken Marsala with Pasta, 79
Chicken Pesto Pizza, 87
Chunky Pasta Sauce, 68
Hearty Spaghetti Sauce, 59
Herbed Mushroom Spaghetti
    Sauce, 66
Italian Sausage-Stuffed Mushrooms, 13
Italian Spinach Salad, 29
Italian Strip Steaks with Focaccia, 78
Mushroom Pork Scallopini, 82
Pasta Primavera, 71
Pesto Sausage Pizza Makeover, 89
Pizza Lover's Pie, 92

Portobellos Parmesano, 36
Roasted Vegetables, 38
Saucy Beef Roast, 81
Spinach Stuffed Pizza, 94
Tuxedo Pasta, 65

nuts (also see Pesto)
Cannoli Cheesecake, 99
Cannoli Cupcakes, 98
Cannoli Pudding, 103
Italian Cream Cake, 105
Sicilian Fig Pastries, 103
Spumoni Slices, 104

olives
Antipasto Medley, 34
Antipasto Salad with Basil
    Dressing, 33
Bacon-Olive Tomato Pizza, 90
Caramelized Onion-Gorgonzola
    Pizza, 86
Chunky Pasta Sauce, 68
Classic Antipasto Platter, 11
Italian Spaghetti Bake, 54
Marinated Pasta Salad, 38
Peppy Parmesan Pasta, 62
Pesto Sausage Pizza Makeover, 89
Pesto Tortellini Salad, 35
Pizza Dip, 8
Prosciutto Bundles, 12
Salami Pasta Salad, 30
Shrimp and Olive Rigatoni, 79
Super Italian Chopped Salad, 38
Tomato & Olive Bread, 32
Tuscan Bean Salad, 37
Tuscan Tossed Salad, 39

onion
Barbecued Chicken Pizza, 93
Caramelized Onion-Gorgonzola
    Pizza, 86
Chicken Fajita Pizza, 92
Rustic Vegetarian Pizza, 93
Sweet Onion 'n' Sausage
    Spaghetti, 59

pasta (also see Potatoes & Gnocchi)
Bow Ties
Four-Cheese Bow Ties, 50
Italian Sausage with Bow Ties, 63
Tuxedo Pasta, 65
Elbow Macaroni
Forgotten Minestrone, 23
Pasta Fagioli Soup, 17
Fettuccine & Linguine
Chicken Marsala with Pasta, 79
Chicken Milan, 83
Fettuccine Primavera, 66
Garden Primavera Fettuccine, 58
Herbed Shrimp Fettuccine, 78
Linguine with Fresh Tomatoes, 71
Parmesan Chicken, 74
Parmesan Noodles, 60
Pasta Primavera, 71
Salmon with Fettuccine
    Alfredo, 74
Seafood Fettuccine, 82
Lasagna
Alfredo Chicken Lasagna, 45

pasta

Lasagna (continued)
Broccoli Chicken Lasagna, 42
Cannelloni, 43
Creamy Chicken Lasagna, 54
Lasagna Rolls, 46
Roasted Vegetable Lasagna, 48
Spinach and Turkey Sausage
    Lasagna, 53
Manicotti
Chicken Spinach Manicotti, 44
Meaty Spinach Manicotti, 52
Overnight Spinach Manicotti, 47
Sausage Broccoli Manicotti, 51
Turkey Manicotti, 55
Orzo
Chicken Orzo Skillet, 70
Ravioli
Beef Ragu with Ravioli, 67
Fried Cheese Ravioli, 13
Ravioli Skillet, 69
Shells
Antipasto Picnic Salad, 28
Italian Stuffed Shells, 49
Makeover Cheese-Stuffed Shells, 48
Marinated Pasta Salad, 38
Salami Pasta Salad, 30
Spinach-Stuffed Shells, 50
Stuffed Shells Florentine, 42
Spaghetti & Angel Hair
Italian Spaghetti and Meatballs, 62
Italian Spaghetti Bake, 54
Peppy Parmesan Pasta, 62
Spaghetti Pie, 47
Sweet Onion 'n' Sausage Spaghetti, 59
Spiral
Pork Italiano, 76
Tuscan Chicken Soup, 21
Tortellini
Alfredo Chicken Tortellini, 69
Chicken Tortellini Soup, 25
Layered Tortellini Salad, 32
Pesto Tortellini Salad, 35
Tortellini Primavera, 60
Tortellini Soup, 19
Tubes (Mostaccioli, Penne,
    Rigatoni, Ziti)
Antipasto Medley, 34
Baked Mostaccioli, 52
Baked Ziti, 43
Baked Ziti with Fresh Tomatoes, 55
Blushing Penne Pasta, 67
Fire-Roasted Ziti with Sausage, 45
Florentine Chicken Soup, 22
Fresh Tomato Pasta Toss, 70
Italian Wedding Soup, 20
Mostaccioli Bake, 49
Penne Sausage Bake, 51
Saucy Beef Roast, 81
Shrimp and Olive Rigatoni, 79
Ziti with Roasted Red Pepper
    Sauce, 61

pasta sauce

Artichoke-Basil Pasta Sauce, 64
Chunky Pasta Sauce, 68
Hearty Spaghetti Sauce, 59
Herbed Mushroom Spaghetti
    Sauce, 66

Italian Pasta Sauce, 61
No-Cook Herbed Tomato Sauce, 71
Slow-Cooked Spaghetti Sauce, 63

pepperoni & turkey pepperoni

Antipasto Medley, 34
Antipasto Picnic Salad, 28
Calzone Pinwheels, 10
Italian Spaghetti Bake, 54
Marinated Pasta Salad, 38
Pepperoni Provolone Pizzas, 88
Peppy Parmesan Pasta, 62
Pizza Dip, 8
Pizza Lover's Pie, 92
Salami Pasta Salad, 30
Stromboli Slices, 12
Super Italian Chopped Salad, 38

peppers

Antipasto Medley, 34
Antipasto Picnic Salad, 28
Antipasto-Stuffed Baguettes, 7
Chicken Fajita Pizza, 92
Chicken Pesto Pizza, 87
Chunky Pasta Sauce, 68
Classic Antipasto Platter, 11
Hearty Italian Sandwiches, 18
Italian Beef Sandwiches, 20
Italian Broccoli with Peppers, 30
Italian Sausage with Peppers, 16
Pasta Primavera, 71
Red Pepper & Parmesan
    Tilapia, 78
Roasted Vegetable Lasagna, 48
Roasted Vegetables, 38
Spinach and Turkey Sausage
    Lasagna, 53
Tuscan Bean Salad, 37
Tuscan Tossed Salad, 39
Ziti with Roasted Red Pepper
    Sauce, 61

pesto

Chicken Pesto Pizza, 87
Pepperoni Provolone Pizzas, 88
Pesto Chicken, 7
Pesto Halibut, 81
Pesto Pizza, 93
Pesto Rice-Stuffed Pork Chops, 77
Pesto Sausage Pizza Makeover, 89
Pesto Swirled Cheesecake, 11
Pesto Tortellini Salad, 35
Tomato Gnocchi with Pesto, 58

pizzas

Alfredo Bacon Mushroom Pizza, 91
Bacon-Olive Tomato Pizza, 90
Baked Potato Pizza, 90
Barbecued Chicken Pizza, 93
Bacon, Lettuce & Tomato Pizza Pie, 95
Caramelized Onion-Gorgonzola
    Pizza, 86
Chicken Fajita Pizza, 92
Chicken Pesto Pizza, 87
Effortless Alfredo Pizza, 89
Homemade Pizza, 86
Pepperoni Provolone Pizzas, 88
Pesto Sausage Pizza Makeover, 89
Pesto Pizza, 93

Pizza Lover's Pie, 92
Rustic Vegetarian Pizza, 93
Shrimp Pizza, 90
Smoked Salmon Pizza, 93
Spinach Stuffed Pizza, 94
Tomato Cheese Pizza, 87
Tomato Spinach Pizza, 91
Turkey Pizza, 94
Two-Meat Pizza, 95

pork

Italian Pork Hoagies, 25
Mushroom Pork Scallopini, 82
Pesto Rice-Stuffed Pork Chops, 77
Pork Italiano, 76

potatoes & gnocchi

Baked Potato Pizza, 90
Gnocchi Chicken Skillet, 64
Gnocchi in Sage Butter, 68
Parmesan Red Potatoes, 36
Tomato Gnocchi with Pesto, 58

prosciutto (also see Ham)

Classic Antipasto Platter, 11
Prosciutto Bundles, 12
Prosciutto Provolone Panini, 21
Ravioli Skillet, 69

rosemary

Beef Ragu with Ravioli, 67
Florentine Chicken Soup, 22
Fresh Herb Flat Bread, 28
Herb Mix for Dipping Oil, 13
Roasted Garlic Bread, 37
Rosemary Cheese Patties, 6
Rosemary Veal Meatballs, 9

salads

Antipasto Medley, 34
Antipasto Picnic Salad, 28
Antipasto Salad with Basil
    Dressing, 33
Fresh Mozzarella Tomato Salad, 36
Italian Spinach Salad, 29
Layered Tortellini Salad, 32
Marinated Pasta Salad, 38
Parmesan Romaine Salad, 31
Pesto Tortellini Salad, 35
Salami Pasta Salad, 30
Super Italian Chopped Salad, 38
Tuscan Bean Salad, 37
Tuscan Tossed Salad, 39

salami

Antipasto Medley, 34
Antipasto Picnic Salad, 28
Antipasto Salad with Basil Dressing, 33
Antipasto-Stuffed Baguettes, 7
Classic Antipasto Platter, 11
Marinated Pasta Salad, 38
Salami Pasta Salad, 30
Super Italian Chopped Salad, 38

sandwiches

Barbecue Italian Sausages, 19
Caprese Sandwiches, 22
Chicken Alfredo Stromboli, 24
Focaccia Sandwich, 22

simply Italian

Hearty Italian Sandwiches, 18
Hearty Sausage Stromboli, 17
Italian Beef Sandwiches, 20
Italian Pork Hoagies, 25
Italian Sausage with Peppers, 16
Meatball Calzones, 24
Monterey Artichoke Panini, 25
Prosciutto Provolone Panini, 21
Spinach Meatball Subs, 23

sausage (*also see Turkey &
Turkey Sausage*)
Barbecue Italian Sausages, 19
Fire-Roasted Ziti with Sausage, 45
Hearty Italian Sandwiches, 18
Hearty Sausage Stromboli, 17
Italian Pasta Sauce, 61
Italian Sausage with Bow Ties, 63
Italian Sausage with Peppers, 16
Italian Wedding Soup, 20
Meaty Spinach Manicotti, 52
Pesto Sausage Pizza Makeover, 89
Pizza Lover's Pie, 92
Sausage Broccoli Manicotti, 51
Tortellini Soup, 19
Two-Meat Pizza, 95

side dishes
Italian Broccoli with Peppers, 30
Parmesan Noodles, 60
Parmesan Red Potatoes, 36
Portobellos Parmesano, 36
Roasted Vegetables, 38

slow cooker recipes
Chicken Cacciatore, 76
Forgotten Minestrone, 23
Hearty Italian Sandwiches, 18
Italian Beef Sandwiches, 20
Pizza Dip, 8
Saucy Beef Roast, 81
Slow-Cooked Spaghetti
    Sauce, 63

soups
Chicken Tortellini Soup, 25
Florentine Chicken Soup, 22
Forgotten Minestrone, 23
Garlic Tomato Soup, 16
Italian Wedding Soup, 20

Pasta Fagioli Soup, 17
Tortellini Soup, 19
Tuscan Chicken Soup, 21

spinach & escarole
Antipasto-Stuffed Baguettes, 7
Cannelloni, 43
Chicken Spinach Manicotti, 44
Effortless Alfredo Pizza, 89
Florentine Chicken Soup, 22
Italian Spinach Salad, 29
Italian Wedding Soup, 20
Layered Tortellini Salad, 32
Makeover Cheese-Stuffed
    Shells, 48
Meaty Spinach Manicotti, 52
Monterey Artichoke Panini, 25
Mostaccioli Bake, 49
Overnight Spinach Manicotti, 47
Pasta Fagioli Soup, 17
Spinach and Turkey Sausage
    Lasagna, 53
Spinach Meatball Subs, 23
Spinach Stuffed Pizza, 94
Spinach-Stuffed Shells, 50
Stuffed Shells Florentine, 42
Tilapia Florentine, 80
Tomato Spinach Pizza, 91
Tuscan Chicken Soup, 21

tomatoes
Antipasto Salad with Basil
    Dressing, 33
Bacon, Lettuce & Tomato Pizza
    Pie, 95
Bacon-Olive Tomato Pizza, 90
Baked Ziti with Fresh Tomatoes, 55
Beef Ragu with Ravioli, 67
Bruschetta Chicken, 82
Caprese Sandwiches, 22
Chunky Pasta Sauce, 68
Cilantro Tomato Bruschetta, 12
Classic Antipasto Platter, 11
Creamy Chicken Lasagna, 54
Fire-Roasted Ziti with Sausage, 45
Four-Cheese Bow Ties, 50
Fresh Mozzarella Tomato Salad, 36
Fresh Tomato Pasta Toss, 70
Garlic Tomato Soup, 16
Hearty Spaghetti Sauce, 59

Italian Pasta Sauce, 61
Italian Spinach Salad, 29
Layered Tortellini Salad, 32
Linguine with Fresh Tomatoes, 71
Marinated Pasta Salad, 38
No-Cook Herbed Tomato Sauce, 71
Parmesan Romaine Salad, 31
Pasta Primavera, 71
Roasted Vegetable Lasagna, 48
Rustic Vegetarian Pizza, 93
Shrimp and Olive Rigatoni, 79
Slow-Cooked Spaghetti Sauce, 63
Smoked Salmon Pizza, 93
Smothered Chicken Italiano, 81
Sweet Onion 'n' Sausage
    Spaghetti, 59
Tomato & Olive Bread, 32
Tomato Cheese Pizza, 87
Tomato Gnocchi with Pesto, 58
Tomato Spinach Pizza, 91
Tortellini Primavera, 60
Tuscan Tossed Salad, 39

turkey & turkey sausage
(*also see Bacon & Turkey Bacon,
Pepperoni & Turkey Pepperoni*)
Effortless Alfredo Pizza, 89
Focaccia Sandwich, 22
Italian Sausage-Stuffed
    Mushrooms, 13
Makeover Cheese-Stuffed Shells, 48
Pasta Fagioli Soup, 17
Penne Sausage Bake, 51
Spinach and Turkey Sausage
    Lasagna, 53
Sweet Onion 'n' Sausage
    Spaghetti, 59
Turkey Manicotti, 55
Turkey Pizza, 94

zucchini & squash
Fettuccine Primavera, 66
Forgotten Minestrone, 23
Garden Primavera Fettuccine, 58
Pasta Primavera, 71
Roasted Vegetable Lasagna, 48
Roasted Vegetables, 38
Rustic Vegetarian Pizza, 93
Tortellini Primavera, 60
Tuxedo Pasta, 65

alphabetical index

a
Alfredo Bacon Mushroom
    Pizza, 91
Alfredo Chicken Lasagna, 45
Alfredo Chicken Tortellini, 69
Antipasto Medley, 34
Antipasto Picnic Salad, 28
Antipasto Salad with Basil
    Dressing, 33
Antipasto-Stuffed Baguettes, 7
Artichoke-Basil Pasta
    Sauce, 64

b
Bacon, Lettuce & Tomato Pizza Pie, 95
Bacon-Olive Tomato Pizza, 90
Baked Mostaccioli, 52
Baked Potato Pizza, 90
Baked Ziti, 43
Baked Ziti with Fresh Tomatoes, 55
Barbecue Italian Sausages, 19
Barbecued Chicken Pizza, 93
Basil-Cheese Bread Strips, 39
Beef Ragu with Ravioli, 67
Blushing Penne Pasta, 67

Broccoli Chicken Lasagna, 42
Bruschetta Chicken, 82

c
Calzone Pinwheels, 10
Cannelloni, 43
Cannoli Cheesecake, 99
Cannoli Cupcakes, 98
Cannoli Pudding, 103
Caprese Sandwiches, 22
Caramelized Onion-Gorgonzola
    Pizza, 86

Cheesy Mushroom Morsels, 9
Chicken Alfredo Stromboli, 24
Chicken Cacciatore, 76
Chicken Fajita Pizza, 92
Chicken Marsala with Pasta, 79
Chicken Milan, 83
Chicken Orzo Skillet, 70
Chicken Parmigiana, 77
Chicken Pesto Pizza, 87
Chicken Piccata, 75
Chicken Spinach Manicotti, 44
Chicken Tortellini Soup, 25
Chocolate Cannoli Cake, 102
Chunky Pasta Sauce, 68
Cilantro Tomato Bruschetta, 12
Classic Antipasto Platter, 11
Creamy Chicken Lasagna, 54

e

Easter Bread, 35
Easy Espresso, 103
Easy Tiramisu, 99
Effortless Alfredo Pizza, 89
Eggplant Parmigiana, 46
Espresso Panna Cotta, 99

f

Fettuccine Primavera, 66
Fire-Roasted Ziti with Sausage, 45
Florentine Chicken Soup, 22
Focaccia Sandwich, 22
Forgotten Minestrone, 23
Four-Cheese Bow Ties, 50
Fresh Herb Flat Bread, 28
Fresh Mozzarella Tomato
    Salad, 36
Fresh Tomato Pasta Toss, 70
Fried Cheese Ravioli, 13

g

Garden Primavera Fettuccine, 58
Garlic Tomato Soup, 16
Genoise with Fruit 'n' Cream
    Filling, 107
Gnocchi Chicken Skillet, 64
Gnocchi in Sage Butter, 68

h

Hearty Italian Sandwiches, 18
Hearty Sausage Stromboli, 17
Hearty Spaghetti Sauce, 59
Herb Mix for Dipping Oil, 13
Herbed Mushroom Spaghetti
    Sauce, 66
Herbed Shrimp Fettuccine, 78
Homemade Pizza, 86

i

Italian Beef Sandwiches, 20
Italian Bread, 35
Italian Bread Twists, 33

Italian Broccoli with Peppers, 30
Italian Cookies, 100
Italian Cream Cake, 105
Italian Dinner Rolls, 31
Italian Lemon Frozen Dessert, 105
Italian Pasta Sauce, 61
Italian Pork Hoagies, 25
Italian Pot Roast, 83
Italian Sausage-Stuffed
    Mushrooms, 13
Italian Sausage with Bow Ties, 63
Italian Sausage with Peppers, 16
Italian Spaghetti and Meatballs, 62
Italian Spaghetti Bake, 54
Italian Spinach Salad, 29
Italian Strip Steaks with Focaccia, 78
Italian Stuffed Shells, 49
Italian Wedding Soup, 20

l

Lasagna Rolls, 46
Layered Tortellini Salad, 32
Lemon 'n' Lime Strawberry Ice, 107
Lemon Gelato, 98
Lemon Ricotta Cheesecake, 102
Linguine with Fresh Tomatoes, 71

m

Makeover Cheese-Stuffed Shells, 48
Marinated Pasta Salad, 38
Mascarpone Cheesecake, 101
Meatball Calzones, 24
Meaty Spinach Manicotti, 52
Monterey Artichoke Panini, 25
Morning Latte, 100
Mostaccioli Bake, 49
Mushroom Pork Scallopini, 82

n

No-Cook Herbed Tomato Sauce, 71

o

Overnight Spinach Manicotti, 47

p

Parmesan Chicken, 74
Parmesan Noodles, 60
Parmesan Red Potatoes, 36
Parmesan Romaine Salad, 31
Pasta Fagioli Soup, 17
Pasta Primavera, 71
Penne Sausage Bake, 51
Pepperoni Provolone Pizzas, 88
Peppy Parmesan Pasta, 62
Pesto Chicken, 7
Pesto Halibut, 81
Pesto Pizza, 93
Pesto Rice-Stuffed Pork Chops, 77
Pesto Sausage Pizza Makeover, 89
Pesto Swirled Cheesecake, 11
Pesto Tortellini Salad, 35
Pizza Dip, 8

Pizza Lover's Pie, 92
Pizzelle, 104
Pork Italiano, 76
Portobellos Parmesano, 36
Prosciutto Bundles, 12
Prosciutto Provolone Panini, 21

r

Ravioli Skillet, 69
Red Pepper & Parmesan Tilapia, 78
Roasted Garlic Bread, 37
Roasted Vegetable Lasagna, 48
Roasted Vegetables, 38
Rosemary Cheese Patties, 6
Rosemary Veal Meatballs, 9
Rustic Vegetarian Pizza, 93

s

Salami Pasta Salad, 30
Salmon with Fettuccine Alfredo, 74
Saucy Beef Roast, 81
Sausage Broccoli Manicotti, 51
Seafood Fettuccine, 82
Shrimp and Olive Rigatoni, 79
Shrimp Pizza, 90
Sicilian Fig Pastries, 103
Slow-Cooked Spaghetti Sauce, 63
Smoked Salmon Pizza, 93
Smothered Chicken Italiano, 81
Spaghetti Pie, 47
Spinach and Turkey Sausage
    Lasagna, 53
Spinach Meatball Subs, 23
Spinach Stuffed Pizza, 94
Spinach-Stuffed Shells, 50
Spumoni Slices, 104
Stromboli Slices, 12
Stuffed Bread Appetizers, 10
Stuffed Shells Florentine, 42
Super Italian Chopped Salad, 38
Sweet Onion 'n' Sausage Spaghetti, 59

t

Tender Italian Sugar Cookies, 106
Tilapia Florentine, 80
Tiramisu, 104
Tiramisu Parfaits, 106
Tomato & Olive Bread, 32
Tomato Cheese Pizza, 87
Tomato Gnocchi with Pesto, 58
Tomato Spinach Pizza, 91
Tortellini Primavera, 60
Tortellini Soup, 19
Turkey Manicotti, 55
Turkey Pizza, 94
Tuscan Bean Salad, 37
Tuscan Chicken Soup, 21
Tuscan Kabobs, 6
Tuscan Tossed Salad, 39
Tuxedo Pasta, 65
Two-Meat Pizza, 95

z

Ziti with Roasted Red Pepper
    Sauce, 61